CONTENTS

PART FOUR
CRITICAL HISTORY

PART FIVE
BACKGROUND

PART ONE

INTRODUCTION

HOW TO STUDY A PLAY

Studying on your own requires self-discipline and a carefully thought-out work plan in order to be effective.

- Drama is a special kind of writing (the technical term is 'genre') because it needs a performance in the theatre to arrive at a full interpretation of its meaning. Try to imagine that you are a member of the audience when reading the play. Think about how it could be presented on the stage, not just about the words on the page.

- Drama is always about conflict of some sort (which may be below the surface). Identify the conflicts in the play and you will be close to identifying the large ideas or themes which bind all the parts together.

- Make careful notes on themes, character, plot and any subplots of the play.

- Why do you like or dislike the characters in the play? How do your feelings towards them develop and change?

- Playwrights find non-realistic ways of allowing an audience to see into the minds and motives of their characters, for example , aside or music. Consider how such dramatic devices are used in the play you are studying.

- Think of the playwright writing the play. Why were these particular arrangements of events, characters and speeches chosen?

- Cite exact sources for all quotations, whether from the text itself or from critical commentaries. Wherever possible find your own examples from the play to back up your opinions.

- Where appropriate, comment in detail on the language of the passage you have quoted.

- Always express your ideas in your own words.

These York Notes offer an introduction to *King Lear* and cannot substitute for close reading of the text and the study of secondary sources.

CONTEXT

It is possible that *King Lear* was thought appropriate for presentation to James I on 26 December 1606 because this was a traditional day for celebrating the Christian virtue of patience, necessary for during hardship.

READING *KING LEAR*

Today, *King Lear* is one of Shakespeare's most frequently performed plays. It is not difficult to see why it attracts actors and directors. The story it has to tell – of an ageing patriarch who goes mad and loses everything after a fatal error of judgement – is a powerful one. We watch the agonising downfall of a man whose life is torn apart. The human issues explored in the play resonate in any age: the conflict between parents and children, sibling rivalry, the painful process of working out who and what you are. The picture we are presented with, of frail, difficult and precarious old age challenged by thrusting youth, has struck a chord with many cultures, not just our own. Many literary traditions have their own versions of the Lear story. As Goethe remarked, 'Every old man is a King Lear'. We all wonder what our twilight years will bring, and struggle to prepare ourselves for death. This play is a particularly stark examination of the ageing process. All the deaths that occur – on and off stage – are violent and brutal. *King Lear* also explores the enduringly compelling struggle between good and evil, issues about power and responsibility, and man's relationship with the universe: in particular, nature and the gods.

Literary critics have been eagerly drawn to *King Lear* too. For many this is Shakespeare's most profound **tragedy**, one of the greatest plays written in any language at any time. It throws up questions which remain as perplexing now as they were to Shakespeare's early critics. We are asked to consider a number of 'big' philosophical questions when we read this play. Is mankind cruel or kind? How do we assess human justice? What are we to make of the presentation of religion in *King Lear*? There are no easy answers to these questions, or to the many others you will find yourself asking as you study the play. *King Lear* is a disturbing read, more shocking in its mental and physical violence than any of Shakespeare's other plays. It pushes its readers, as its central character is pushed, to consider the nature of suffering and the human condition. *King Lear* also offers many opportunities to indulge in the two emotions **Aristotle** defined as necessary in tragedy: pity and fear. This play is both exhausting and exhilarating. Audiences and readers alike find its relentlessness deeply moving.

CHECK THE BOOK

For a detailed discussion of the historical context of the performance of *King Lear* that Shakespeare's company gave for James I in 1606, see Leah Marcus' essay 'Retrospective: *King Lear* on St Stephen's Night, 1606' in *King Lear: A Casebook*, ed. Kiernan Ryan, 1993.

THE PLOT AND ITS SOURCES

King Lear has a double plot; a main plot and a subplot. The story of Gloucester and his sons heightens the tragedy that occurs in the main plot and provides points of comparison with the royal family. The main focus, however, is the tragic protagonist, Lear. His foolishness and suffering absorb us most. Lear is a symbolic figure who represents England. In *King Lear* Shakespeare explores what happens when the realm is plunged into crisis, focusing on the consequences of the actions of two rash patriarchs. The action unfolds swiftly. By the end of the first scene the kingdom has been divided and Lear's family harmony is shattered. Thereafter the descent into chaos gathers pace, culminating in a final scene of dramatic and violent death.

When seeking source material for his play Shakespeare probably turned to the historian Holinshed's *Chronicles of England, Scotland and Ireland* (1577), which he had used before. There were also accounts of Lear's reign in a sentimental play of the 1590s, *The True Chronicle History of King Leir*, Spenser's great poem *The Faerie Queen* and in John Higgins' *A Mirror for Magistrates*. *The True Chronicle History of King Leir* had a 'happy ending', with Lear restored to his throne. Shakespeare might have found his subplot in Sidney's prose romance *Arcadia*. Sidney tells the story of a blind Paphalogian king with two sons, one of whom plots against him. When he realises the truth about his evil son, the king wishes to throw himself from a cliff.

Finally, Shakespeare was probably familiar with two 'real life' Lear stories. During his early life in London a former mayor of the city, Sir William Allen, divided his property between his three daughters. His decision proved to be disastrous, for he was badly treated by all his offspring. There was also the case of Sir Brian Annesley, a gentleman pensioner of Elizabeth I. In 1603 his eldest daughter and her husband tried to have the old man certified as a senile lunatic, so that they could take control of his property. His youngest daughter Cordell saved the day by challenging her sister in court.

> **CONTEXT**
>
> The Lear story had been popular since the Middle Ages, and there had been a previous stage version in the 1590s – *The True Chronicle History of King Leir*.

CHECK THE NET
www.absolute shakespeare.com/ guides for Lear context and character reviews.

By considering Shakespeare's changes and additions to the Lear story and his use of the Gloucester subplot, it is possible to see where the playwright's dramatic interests lie. Lear's madness is Shakespeare's invention, as is the manner of Cordelia's death. It seems that Shakespeare is intent on producing an impression of bleakness.

PART TWO

THE TEXT

NOTE ON THE TEXT

It is not possible to date the composition of *King Lear* exactly, but it is thought that the play was written between late 1605 and early 1606. There was a performance of the play at court in late 1606, although it is unlikely that this was the first performance. *King Lear* probably had its first outing at The Globe Theatre, like many of Shakespeare's other plays. A greater problem exists in trying to decide which version of *King Lear* to accept as the most authentic 'Shakespearean' text. The first published version of *King Lear* appeared in 1608 (the First Quarto). There are various theories about how the Quarto text was arrived at. It has been suggested that the First Quarto was produced by a printer with the assistance of the boy actors who played Gonerill and Regan, who also had access to a rough draft of the play. Only half of Shakespeare's plays were published in the playwright's lifetime in the paperback Quarto format, and not all of these Quartos were based on authentic manuscripts. They are thus 'unauthorised' versions of Shakespeare's plays. After the playwright's death, all of Shakespeare's works were prepared for publication as the First Folio of 1623. It has been suggested that the Folio was based on a revised prompt book copy of *King Lear*. It also seems likely that this cut Folio text represents the version of the play that was performed successfully, after the play's initial performances in 1605–6.

The problem is this: the Quarto and Folio versions of *King Lear* differ quite radically in parts. The Quartos omit approximately a hundred lines which are found in the Folio, while the Folio does not include three hundred lines of the Quarto. The main omissions in the Folio include Lear's 'mock trial' of Gonerill in the hovel during Act III, the sympathetic dialogue between Cornwall's two servants following Gloucester's blinding, and all of Act IV Scene 3 where the Gentleman describes Cordelia's grief. The end of the final scene of the play, including Lear's final speech, is also different in the two texts. Stanley Wells and Gary Taylor, the editors of the Oxford *The*

> **CONTEXT**
>
> St Stephen's Night, which is now called Boxing Day, was traditionally associated with hospitality to the poor and homeless. This play, in which the sovereign is reduced to a beggar, was therefore an apt choice for performance at court during Christmas 1606.

CONTEXT
Prior to the permanent establishment of acting companies in London in the late sixteenth century, almost all plays were written for performance on specific holy days.

Complete Works of Shakespeare, feel that the mood of the revised Folio text of *King Lear* is less reflective. The Folio version is also bleaker and more pessimistic. So which is the version of the play which most closely reflects Shakespeare's dramatic intentions? It is very difficult to say. We cannot be sure that Shakespeare himself made the revisions found in the Folio – since no texts of *King Lear* survive in the playwright's handwriting.

Most modern editions of *King Lear* are based on the Folio, with the missing Quarto lines restored. However, Wells and Taylor suggest that the two versions of *King Lear* deserve consideration as separate plays, and present both the Quarto and Folio texts in their *The Complete Works*. It is certainly worth looking at both versions of *King Lear*. You should also check to see which version(s) of *King Lear* your own play text is based on.

For a more detailed discussion of the Quarto and Folio versions of *King Lear* and the differences in the Quarto and Folio texts, see Kenneth Muir's introduction to the play in the Arden edition, and Stanley Wells and Gary Taylor's *The Complete Works*. See Further Reading for information about these editions of *King Lear*.

The edition used in these Notes is the Penguin Edition of *King Lear*, edited by G.K. Hunter.

SYNOPSIS

Reaching old age and desiring a quiet life without the responsibilities and cares of state, King Lear decides to divide his kingdom between his three daughters, Gonerill, Regan and Cordelia. He devises a 'love-test' to see which daughter loves him most, expecting his favourite youngest daughter Cordelia to 'win' and claim the largest share of the kingdom. Cordelia thwarts his plan, refusing to take part in the 'love-test'. Furious, Lear casts her off and divides the kingdom between Gonerill and Regan. Cordelia marries the King of France, and leaves Britain. Gonerill and Regan decide to rid themselves of their tiresome father once and for all, and plot against Lear. They drive him out into a storm and shut the doors against him. Alone on the heath except for two faithful servants (Kent and the Fool) and a counterfeit mad beggar (Poor Tom), Lear goes mad. Meanwhile, his friend the Earl of Gloucester has also been treated treacherously by his illegitimate son Edmund, who has duped him into believing his legitimate son Edgar seeks his life. Attempting to help Lear, Gloucester incurs the wrath of Lear's daughters and is blinded as a punishment. Learning from letters of her father's plight, Cordelia returns to Britain with the French army. She intends restoring Lear to his throne. Lear and Cordelia are reunited at the French camp in Dover. The French and British armies clash in battle. The French army loses. Lear and Cordelia are imprisoned by Edmund. Gonerill and Regan have both been rivals for Edmund's love, and their lust drives the sisters to desperate behaviour. Gonerill poisons Regan and then kills herself. Meanwhile Edmund has ordered Lear and Cordelia's deaths. In spite of the efforts of Gonerill's husband Albany to save them, Cordelia is hanged in prison. Her death is too much for Lear, who has come to a greater understanding of himself and others through his madness. Lear dies a broken man, half mad.

ACT I

SCENE 1

- Lear divests himself of the cares of state using a 'love-test'.
- Cordelia and Kent are banished for displeasing him.
- The kingdom is divided between Gonerill and Regan.

The play opens at Lear's court. Kent and Gloucester discuss the division of the kingdom. There are rumours about King Lear's intentions towards his two sons-in-law, the dukes of Albany and Cornwall. Kent suggests that Lear has favoured the Duke of Albany up to now. Gloucester introduces his illegitimate son Edmund to Kent. We learn that Edmund has been 'out nine years, and away he / shall again' (lines 31–2). We also learn that Gloucester has another legitimate son, and that he favours both sons equally.

CONTEXT

Inheritance issues were a matter of national concern for Shakespeare's audience in the late sixteenth and early seventeenth centuries; Elizabeth I was unmarried and childless.

QUESTION

How effective is
Act I Scene 1 as an
opening to the
play?

Lear enters with his three daughters, Gonerill, Regan and Cordelia, and Gonerill and Regan's husbands, Albany and Cornwall. He announces that he has divided his kingdom in three and intends to distribute it between his daughters. He wants to 'shake all cares and business from our age' (line 39) and pass the responsibility of ruling on to his children. However, he also wishes to retain the 'Pre-eminence, and all the large effects / That troop with majesty' (lines 131–2). In order to determine who should enjoy the largest share of the kingdom, Lear asks his daughters to take part in a ceremonial 'love-test'. The daughter who says she loves him most will be the 'winner'.

Gonerill speaks first. She says she loves her father more than 'eyesight, space, and liberty' (line 56). Regan emphasises the value of her love; she should be priced at Gonerill's 'worth'. Cordelia dislikes her sisters' 'ponderous' (line 78) words and hopes that she will be able to speak of her love more honestly and simply. She refuses to take part in Lear's 'contest' and says she has 'nothing' to say, except that she loves Lear as her duty instructs her. Lear is hurt and angry. He urges Cordelia to speak again. When she refuses to obey him, he casts her off without a moment's hesitation. Kent attempts to argue with the king, accusing him of 'hideous rashness' (line 151). He also warns Lear that Gonerill and Regan are false flatterers. Further enraged, Lear banishes Kent too. He then calls for Cordelia's two suitors, France and Burgundy and invests Albany and Cornwall with power. We learn that he intends keeping one hundred knights in his service, who will accompany him as he divides his time between Gonerill and Regan.

Burgundy politely refuses to take Cordelia's hand in marriage unless Lear provides the dowry he had promised previously. France takes her – penniless and without her father's favour – for her virtues alone. He leads Cordelia away. An urgent discussion between Gonerill and Regan closes the scene. Gonerill resolves that the sisters 'must do something, and i'th'heat' (line 306). They complain about Lear's rash judgement and unpredictable behaviour and say they are worried that they will receive unfair treatment, like their sister Cordelia.

COMMENTARY

A mood of uncertainty is established in the first six lines of the play, which are typical of Elizabethan and Jacobean drama, where characters set the scene and introduce key themes and ideas. We learn that inheritance and property issues are at stake in *King Lear* when Kent and Gloucester discuss the division of the kingdom. Ideas about favouritism are also introduced in the opening exchange. Edmund's silence is significant. It is symbolic of his position as the bastard son, who has no 'voice', rights or position in society. Shakespeare keeps Edmund's true character concealed at this point, so that his opening **soliloquy** in the next scene is exciting and surprising. Edmund's polite exterior conceals his evil nature, suggesting that the difference between appearances and reality is a key theme in this play. Gloucester takes his rule of Edmund for granted, shown by the brief (some would say brutal) lines he speaks about Edmund's past and future. However, we should not assume that Gloucester is embarrassed by his illegitimate offspring. He jokes easily about Edmund's bastardy, suggesting that he has rather lax morals. Questions about family relationships are raised.

Lear's entrance is impressive, suggesting his power. But we question his use of that power almost immediately. His 'love-test' is foolish and egotistical, as is his desire to be treated as an important, royal personage after he has given away his kingdom. We should also be alarmed by Lear's intention to break up his state. His actions are not those of a responsible ruler. In Act I Scene 1 Lear shows many times that he is most concerned with appearances, and does not see clearly. He is fooled by Gonerill and Regan's superficial and elegant speeches and fails to recognise Cordelia and Kent's honesty. Cordelia stands up for genuine feeling and the correct order in family life when she says that some of her love should go to her husband when she marries. Her strength of character and integrity are shown again when she scorns Burgundy and parts frostily from her sisters, telling them that she knows they are cunning and false. However, some commentators see Lear's youngest daughter as stubborn and destructive (like her father?). There is a troubling irony in the fact that it is Cordelia who rebels against Lear first. Kent is also subversive in this scene. He uses insulting language when he refers to Lear as 'thou' and 'old man' (line 146). However, we understand that Cordelia and Kent have Lear – and England's – best interests at heart. They hope to alert Lear to his false, materialistic values.

Lear behaves like a tyrant in Act I Scene 1. However, we know he has lost control when he goes to strike Kent. He continues to issue orders, and speaks very cruelly to Cordelia, but his authority has been denied. It is possible to feel some sympathy for the king, in spite of his rash behaviour. He clearly loved his youngest daughter a great deal, dividing the kingdom so that she would receive the most opulent share, hoping he could rely on her 'kind nursery' (line 124) as he 'crawls' (line 41) towards death (his language here suggests the vulnerability of a baby). He is pained and humiliated by Cordelia's refusal to take part in his 'love-test'. Nonetheless, we are likely to recognise the truth of Gonerill and Regan's remarks about their father at the end of the scene. They sum up the explosive, violent Lear we have just seen. Can we trust these two though? Perhaps Gonerill and Regan simply justify the wicked intentions they already possess when they decide to 'hit together' (line 302). By the end of this scene family and national harmony have been destroyed. One daughter has challenged her father, and two more prepare to subvert his authority. Lear's tragic fall proceeds from his misuse of power in Act I Scene 1.

CONTEXT

The love contest in Act I Scene 1 has been compared to those enacted in fairy tales and folklore.

GLOSSARY	
81	**validity** value, worth
85	**interested** admitted to, joined with (giving the man who marries Cordelia an advantage in life)
110	**Hecat** Hecate, goddess of night, darkness, the underworld, and witchcraft
114	**Propinquity and property of blood** close family ties, kinship
116	**Scythian** savage; Scythians who lived in an area of Russia were thought to be a barbaric, cruel people, given to cannibalism
117	**makes his generation messes** continuing the theme of barbaric cannibalism; he who feeds on his own children
136	**th' addition** honours and titles
136	**sway** control

160	Apollo in Roman mythology, the god of the Sun
178	Jupiter the Roman ruler of the gods
202	infirmities she owes faults or disabilities she possesses
206	Election makes not up in such conditions it is not possible to make a choice in these circumstances
231	still soliciting constantly looking for favours
235	tardiness in nature natural reticence
268	washed tearful; there is the sense that Cordelia sees clearly what her sisters are like, through 'washed eyes'

Scene 2

- Edmund makes his father Gloucester believe that Edgar seeks his life.

Alone on stage, Edmund offers his view of life. He refuses to submit to the patriarchal hierarchy we saw in operation in Act I Scene 1. Instead, he declares that nature is his goddess. He argues that he possesses personal qualities that make him his legitimate brother's equal. Why should he be denied property and power because he is illegitimate? Edmund is determined to 'grow' and 'prosper' (line 21). Like Gonerill and Regan, he is ready to defend his own interests. He has written a letter which he intends to use to gain advantage over Edgar. At this point in the play he seeks to inherit his brother's land.

Gloucester comes in muttering, disturbed by Lear's rashness. He notices Edmund putting away his letter and asks to see it. Edmund pretends that he is reluctant to allow his father to see the letter, which is supposedly from Edgar. Gloucester is alarmed by what he reads. 'Edgar' suggests that he is unhappy because he wants to enjoy Gloucester's fortunes now, and feels frustrated by the 'idle and fond bondage' of 'aged tyranny' (line 49). He seems to be suggesting that he wishes his father dead, so that he and Edmund can enjoy half of

CONTEXT

Edmund is a victim of the law of primogeniture, a traditional method of passing on wealth and property. Primogeniture meant that the first-born son inherited the family fortune and his father's titles. As an illegitimate son, Edmund is entitled to nothing.

Gloucester's revenue each. Edmund makes his father even more suspicious by telling him that he heard Edgar say that 'sons at perfect age and fathers declined, the father should be as ward to the son, and the son manage his revenue' (lines 73–5). Appalled, Gloucester demands that his legitimate son be 'apprehended' (line 79) immediately. Edmund pretends to be concerned about family honour and suggests that Gloucester should wait to hear Edgar condemn himself out of his own mouth before taking action. Gloucester agrees to let Edmund 'Frame the business' (line 98) of discovering the truth about Edgar's feelings. Gloucester then reflects pessimistically on the conflict in the nation. He mentions predictions of discord, treason, friendships cooling and fathers and sons going against the 'bias of nature' (line 111). He promises Edmund that he will gain by uncovering Edgar's villainy.

Alone again, Edmund rejects his father's superstitious beliefs. He says that 'whoremaster man' (lines 126–7) is responsible for his own fortunes and actions. He sees Edgar coming and pretends to be musing on the effects of the recent eclipses. The brothers joke about Edmund's supposed fondness for astronomy. Edmund then tells Edgar that he has offended their father and advises him to keep out of Gloucester's way. Edgar is alarmed by this and fears that 'Some villain hath done me wrong' (line 162). Edmund suggests that Edgar go into hiding at his lodgings. His brother falls in with this plan.

COMMENTARY

Edmund's opening **soliloquy** at the beginning of Act I Scene 2 shows the reasoning of the discontented **malcontent**. His last line also reveals his defiance: 'Now gods stand up for bastards' (line 22). However, we quickly realise that Edmund does not need the gods to help him. He is a master manipulator and a fine actor, who takes his father and brother in with disturbing ease. Cold and calculating himself, Edmund preys on the emotions of his relatives in this scene. His view that men make or mar their own fortunes seems entirely plausible at this stage in the play. In Act I Scene 1 and Act I Scene 2 fathers misjudge their children, precipitating their own ruin. Gloucester's swift rejection of Edgar mirrors Lear's rejection of

> **CONTEXT**
>
> The references to astrology and pagan gods in the play remind us that Lear is set in the pre-Christian era. Gloucester's concerns about breaches in nature also reflect Elizabethan and Jacobean beliefs about witchcraft and magic.

Cordelia in the previous scene, while Edmund's villainy prepares the way for Gonerill and Regan's treachery in the next act. The subplot mirrors the Lear plot in other ways. Gloucester is taken in by false words and appearances, just as Lear was. Gloucester's family harmony is now in jeopardy, and inheritance issues are revealed as troublesome here too. Another innocent and virtuous child is cast off, while the father promises property to his unworthy offspring in return for a show of affection. Gloucester puts himself in his son Edmund's power, just as Lear resigned his authority to Gonerill and Regan. Edmund's triumphant opportunism, energy and directness when he is alone on stage mirror Gonerill and Regan's urgent plain-speaking at the end of Act I Scene 1. The evil children are gaining ground.

> **CONTEXT**
>
> The malcontent was a scornful, mocking outsider. John Marston's play, *The Malcontent* established this character as a theatrical type.

GLOSSARY

4	**curiosity of nations** patriarchal laws or rules
25	**Confined to exhibition** given only a small allowance to live on
26	**Upon the gad** suddenly, impulsively
62	**character** handwriting
98	**Wind he unto him** wheedle his intentions out of him
111	**bias of nature** natural tendencies
129	**Ursa Major** a cluster of stars, The Great Bear (those born under it were thought to be lecherous)
133	**catastrophe of the old comedy** in old-fashioned comedies events seemed to be worked out in a mechanical way, with a convenient event or incident of some kind e.g. a timely 'catastrophe' to bring about the denouement. The implication is that Edgar arrives at a convenient time for Edmund
146	**diffidences** mistrust
149	**sectary astronomical** follower or student of astrology

SCENE 3

- Gonerill complains to her steward Oswald about Lear and his followers.

A short space of time has elapsed. Lear is now staying with Gonerill. She complains to her steward Oswald about Lear and his knights. She says that Lear has continued to act erratically, setting everyone at odds. Gonerill is determined to put a stop to this, 'I'll not endure it! … I will not speak to him' (lines 6–9). Oswald hears Lear returning from hunting and Gonerill instructs him to put on a 'weary negligence' (line 13) and tell the other servants to follow suit. She wants to provoke a clash with her father. Gonerill leaves to write a letter to Regan. Presumably she will recount Lear's recent 'gross' (line 5) crimes. Oswald is sent to prepare dinner.

www. CHECK THE NET
www.sparknotes. com/shakespeare/ lear provides context, character analysis and explanations of short and long quotations from the play.

COMMENTARY

How seriously should we take Gonerill's complaints about Lear and his knights? It depends partly on how a director chooses to portray the knights in the next scene. It is possible to suggest that they are a rabble, and that Gonerill is justified in her irritation. But equally, because we know that Gonerill and Regan have been scheming (letters have already been sent back and forth), these complaints look suspiciously empty. It is also worth considering the duties of the host when judging Gonerill's anger. As Lear's host, Gonerill has a duty to protect her father and behave graciously towards him. Instead she prepares to subvert his authority. Throughout this scene her tone is assertive and uncompromising; she insists that she is the wronged party, suggesting that the balance of power is shifting from Lear to his daughters.

GLOSSARY

21	checks punishments, rebukes
27	course lead, example

- Lear and Gonerill clash.
- Lear leaves to stay with Regan.

Lear returns from hunting to find Caius (Kent in disguise), a serving man who seeks employment. He agrees to take him on if he likes him 'no worse after dinner' (line 41). As he calls for food and his Fool, Oswald wanders in and out, following Gonerill's instructions with admirable precision. Lear is enraged and sends one of his knights to bring the insolent wretch back. There is a discussion about the 'great abatement of kindness' (line 59) shown to the king. Both Lear and his followers have noticed that Gonerill's servants have started to treat them unkindly. Lear decides to 'look further into't' (line 70) and asks again for his Fool. We learn that the Fool has been pining away since Cordelia went to France. Lear snaps, 'No more of that' (line 74). He cannot bear to hear his youngest daughter's name mentioned.

When Oswald returns (of his own accord) Lear rages at him, 'Who am I, sir?' Oswald replies insolently, 'My lady's father' (lines 77–8). The king curses and strikes him and Kent trips the 'clotpoll' (line 46) up, earning the king's praise. At this point the Fool makes his first appearance. He offers Kent his coxcomb 'for taking one's part that's out of favour' (line 99). The Fool harps on Lear's folly in riddles and songs. A lot of his lines refer directly to property, the implication being that without his property Lear is helpless. The Fool also suggests that Lear has reversed the natural order. Lear threatens to have him whipped.

Gonerill comes in frowning and launches her own attack on Lear. She accuses him of encouraging quarrelsome behaviour in his knights and suggests that a remedy must be sought. Lear is incredulous. Gonerill continues her verbal assault, complaining about the knights' degeneracy. Lear tries to dismiss these insults but his eldest daughter remains firm; if Lear does not cut down his train, she will. Lear's response to Gonerill's audacious threats is to call his

> **CONTEXT**
>
> In Shakespeare's playhouse, the Fool would have addressed the audience from the downstage area. This would have encouraged the audience to identify with his point of view.

train together and leave. He curses Gonerill and says he still has one 'kind and comfortable' (line 303) daughter left to go to (Regan). At this point Albany enters. Lear appeals to him rather helplessly and carries on cursing Gonerill. Albany is puzzled by Lear's passion and distress. Lear kneels and calls on 'Nature' to help him. He hopes Gonerill will either be sterile or give birth to a thankless child who will torment her. He rushes out. Albany seems shocked, but Gonerill is unperturbed. Lear returns briefly, bewildered to find that that fifty of his followers have already been dismissed (there seems to be an inconsistency in the text here; there are further references to Lear's hundred knights later in this scene and in Act II Scene 4). Lear threatens to take back the power he has given away. He refuses to weep and insists that Regan will help him.

After her father has gone Gonerill continues to complain about Lear's followers and how her father 'holds our lives at mercy' (line 324) all the time he retains them. Albany is uneasy but does not assert himself. He says that they should wait to see what happens. Gonerill sends Oswald to Regan with a letter, presumably describing the course she has taken with Lear and asking for her sister's support.

COMMENTARY

This is a difficult scene for Lear, who finds his expectations and beliefs thwarted at every turn. He is challenged directly by Gonerill, and his dependant state is revealed when Oswald tells him that he is now simply his mistress's father, not a royal monarch who must be obeyed. The Fool's scathing jests also suggest Lear's powerlessness. The fact that he continues to take verbal swipes at Lear after he has been threatened with whipping reinforces the idea that Lear is no longer in control, as does the king's frantic to-ing and fro-ing at the end of the scene. Lear himself begins to question his identity in this scene when he asks 'Who is there that can tell me who I am?' (line 226). His use of 'I' is at odds with the royal 'we' he invokes in his earlier question, 'Are you our daughter?' (line 214). Lear thinks – or hopes – that he is joking when he asks these questions, but the audience will recognise that these are serious concerns, that Lear is no longer omnipotent. Even servants disobey him now. These

CONTEXT

It has been suggested that the same actor probably played the Fool and Cordelia in early productions. This would perhaps explain why the two characters do not appear in the same scenes. Doubling of this kind was common.

questions also reveal Lear's blindness, although there is an indication that he realises he has behaved unwisely when he says, 'Woe that too late repents' (line 251) and calls out in anguish, 'O Lear, Lear, Lear! / Beat at this gate that let thy folly in / And thy dear judgement out!' (lines 266–7).

The dismissal of Lear's knights is significant for a number of reasons. His followers are a symbol of Lear's might and importance, but they also represent real fighting power. With only the support of a few old men, Lear will not be able to assert himself or regain control of the kingdom. His threats and curses seem increasingly empty as the scene unfolds. His speeches become increasingly disjointed as he becomes more distressed, hinting at the madness to come.

Their different responses to Lear suggest that Gonerill and Albany will clash later in the play. Gonerill is more assertive than her husband at this point. Albany's feeble protestations seem inadequate, and suggest that evil will go unchecked for some time to come. Gonerill has assumed control in the main plot in the same ruthless way Edmund deals with his father and brother in the subplot.

CONTEXT

The theatrical convention of the impenetrable disguise was frequently used in Jacobean drama. Audiences accepted that characters would not recognise someone in disguise. There are many examples of important characters who adopt a disguise in Shakespeare's plays; for example, in *Measure for Measure*, Duke Vincentio pretends to be a friar so that he can spy on his people incognito. In *King Lear*, Edgar and Kent are forced to conceal their identities to preserve their lives.

GLOSSARY

4	razed disguised, changed
94	earnest part of Kent's wage, a token payment
110	Lady Brach name of a female dog, bitch, who flatters the master and is allowed to sit by the fire
185	frontlet frown
196	all licensed fool who is given the freedom to say anything
201	redress remedies
206	wholesome weal well-being of the state
291	at a clap in one go
297	untented untreated, untreatable
322	buzz rumour

Scene 5

- Lear sends a letter to Regan.
- He fears he is going mad.

Lear sends Kent to deliver a letter to Regan, announcing his arrival. Kent is not to tell Regan anything about the events of the previous scene. Presumably Lear wants to offer his own account of Gonerill's heartless disobedience. The Fool continues to make barbed comments about Lear's predicament. Lear says that he has wronged Cordelia. He fears that Gonerill's ingratitude is driving him mad and wonders if he can reclaim his throne by violent means. A knight informs Lear that his horses are ready.

COMMENTARY

This scene, which appropriately takes place outside, suggests Lear's growing isolation and increasingly fragile mental state. Lear is so distracted by disturbing thoughts that he hardly engages with the Fool. His recognition that he has mistreated Cordelia increases the sense of isolation. We already suspect that Regan will receive him coldly. Soon Lear will have no one to turn to; he will be isolated from all of his daughters. Perhaps he is anxious about the reception he will receive from Regan too; is this why he does not mention the events of Act I Scene 4 in his letter? Lear is still blind to a number of truths, however. He does not recognise his faults as a father (in his view, his troubles are all caused by his ungrateful offspring), and we know he has little chance of reclaiming the throne now. After the tension and violent emotions of Act I Scene 5, the Fool's vulgar rhyming couplet which closes the scene comes as a moment of light relief. An interval (however short) is welcome; we know that Lear's suffering has started in earnest.

CONTEXT

Elizabethan and Jacobean dramatists often employed minor characters to reveal important information or ideas. The Fool fits into this tradition because he offers a commentary on significant events whenever he is on stage.

GLOSSARY

9	kibes chilblains
12	slipshod wearing slippers

ACT II

SCENE 1

- Edmund persuades Edgar to flee.
- Gloucester issues orders to have Edgar hunted down.
- Regan and Cornwall arrive at Gloucester's castle.

The scene now moves to the Great Hall of Gloucester's castle. Curan informs Edmund that Cornwall and Regan are expected soon. There is gossip concerning 'likely wars' (line 10) between Cornwall and Albany, suggesting further strife between brothers. Edmund determines to use Cornwall and Regan's arrival to his own advantage. He calls Edgar down from his hiding place and tells him he must escape at once. He asks Edgar whether he has spoken against Cornwall, implying that Cornwall and Regan are as enraged against him as Gloucester. Alarmed, Edgar denies abusing Cornwall. Edgar is drawn into a mock fight with Edmund, and then flees. Edmund deliberately wounds himself. He cries out for help, and Gloucester rushes in. He sends his servants to pursue Edgar.

Edmund paints a very black picture of his brother. He says that Edgar tried to involve him in a plan to murder Gloucester. He pretends that his wound was caused by Edgar. Gloucester is fooled, horrified by the idea of a son who appears to have broken all the natural bonds between father and child. He says that Edgar will be caught, no matter how far he goes. When he is caught he will be executed. Anyone who helps Edgar will also die. Edmund reports a conversation he alleges to have had with his brother. He says that Edgar mocked his bastardy; who would take the word of the illegitimate child against the legitimate one?

A trumpet announces the arrival of Cornwall and Regan. Gloucester praises Edmund as a 'loyal and natural boy' (line 83) and says he will disinherit Edgar. Cornwall and Regan have already been told the 'strange news' (line 86) of Edgar's treachery. Regan wonders whether Edgar was egged on to thoughts of patricide by

CHECK THE FILM

The television version of the National Theatre production starring Ian Holm as Lear characterises Edmund as a malcontent scientist – interested in optics and technology – as a symbol for the generation gap between him and his superstitious father Gloucester.

Lear's riotous knights. She has received Gonerill's letter, which gives details of the knights' unruly behaviour. Like Gonerill, Regan has no intention of giving them house room (this is the real reason why she and Cornwall have come to visit Gloucester). Cornwall praises Edmund for showing his father 'a child-like office' (line 105). Regan says she wants advice about how to answer the letters she has received. Edmund promises to serve Cornwall.

COMMENTARY

CONTEXT

As well as being discontented, Edmund is also **Machiavellian**. Shakespeare's contemporaries misunderstood the works of the influential Florentine writer, Niccolo Machiavelli. They believed that Machiavelli proposed that rulers should behave in immoral and corrupt ways. Edmund's Machiavellian, immoral practices include his deception, betrayal and sexual misconduct.

In this scene we see the evil characters continue to gain ground. Edmund's plans prosper and he now aligns himself with Cornwall and Regan; plot and subplot become intertwined. Edmund's quick wits help him here. He is able to respond to events, as well as control them. His lines to Edgar at the start of the scene are full of short, sharp statements and questions, suggesting his command of circumstances. He achieves the goal he set himself in Act I Scene 2 with terrifying ease, indicating how effortlessly evil begins to run riot in the kingdom. Gloucester follows Edmund's lead entirely and appears to be overwhelmed. Like Lear, he seems vulnerable, indicated by his speech to Regan; 'my old heart is cracked, it's cracked' (line 89). Thoughts of filial ingratitude distress both patriarchs now. Gloucester is also isolated in this scene. As the evil characters draw closer together, he has little to say. Regan and Cornwall are as smooth and assured as Edmund. Both assume a commanding tone. Regan's comforting and affectionate words to Gloucester are perhaps surprising. Shakespeare is leaving her true nature partially concealed, for maximum dramatic impact in Act II Scene 4. However, we are likely to distrust her; she and Gonerill share the same low opinion of Lear's followers, and Regan has deliberately chosen to thwart her father's plans by coming to visit Gloucester. Essentially, she is denying her father shelter. When Edmund offers his services to Cornwall we will be alarmed; what is the bastard son hoping to gain now?

GLOSSARY		
8	ear kissing	whispered
17	queasy	delicate, sensitive, difficult
49	in fell motion	with a hard cruel thrust

54	gasted scared
64	pight fixed, determined
66	unpossessing as a bastard, Edmund has no property or inheritance rights, he possesses nothing
72	practice intriguing, scheming
76	fastened firmly decided, resolute

SCENE 2

- Kent quarrels with Oswald and challenges him to a fight.
- He is punished by Cornwall, who puts him in the stocks.

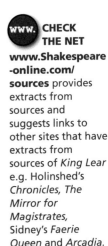

CHECK THE NET
www.Shakespeare -online.com/ **sources** provides extracts from sources and suggests links to other sites that have extracts from sources of *King Lear* e.g. Holinshed's *Chronicles, The Mirror for Magistrates,* Sidney's *Faerie Queen* and *Arcadia*.

The two messengers, Kent/Caius and Oswald, meet outside Gloucester's castle. Kent immediately quarrels with Oswald, accusing him of being a conceited coward (amongst other things). Oswald is perplexed by Kent's aggression. He fails to recognise his adversary. When Kent challenges him to fight, Oswald shows his true colours; he backs away and yells out for help. His cries bring Edmund, Cornwall, Regan, Gonerill and servants running. Edmund tries to part the combatants, but Kent is keen to give Oswald a beating. Cornwall stops the fight. When asked why he dislikes Oswald so much, Kent says his face offends him. Unable to hold his tongue, he then insults Cornwall.

Kent is placed in the stocks as a punishment for his plain-speaking. He protests that he is on the king's business, and should not be treated in this degrading fashion. Cornwall ignores him and says that Kent will be left in the stocks until noon. Regan says he should be left there all night. When Gloucester tries to plead for Kent, Cornwall sweeps his protestations aside. Gloucester stays behind to offer his condolences to Kent. He tries to excuse Cornwall. Kent is stoical and says he'll 'sleep out' (line 154) his time in the stocks. Alone on stage he reveals that he has a letter from Cordelia. She intends to put right all the wrongs that have been done to Lear since she was banished.

CHECK THE FILM

Laurence Olivier's performance of *King Lear* televised in 1980 emphasises the pre-Christian setting of the play. It opens within the stone circle of Stonehenge. Lear enters, leaning heavily on his favourite daughter, as the rest of the court prostrate themselves before him.

COMMENTARY

The audience will enjoy Kent's long list of imaginative and lively insults. Oswald is a worthy object of scorn and the quarrel at the start of the scene provides a moment of relief. Behind Kent's insults lies a serious point; the dangers of the bad servant. It is possible to argue that *King Lear* is full of bad servants, who subvert the order that they should be serving faithfully. Kent also makes a serious point when he says he does not like the faces he sees before him; unlike Lear, he is not fooled by appearances and recognises Cornwall, Regan and Oswald for what they are. He voices the concerns of the audience when he insults Cornwall. However, Kent is punished again for his goodness and honesty, as Cordelia and Edgar have been punished, in spite of their virtues. The punishment of Kent is significant for other reasons. We see that Cornwall is arrogant, Regan vindictive. It becomes clear that husband and wife operate effectively as a team and enjoy their cruelty, hinting at the horrors to come in Act III Scene 7. It is also clear that power is in new hands. Gloucester is ineffectual in this scene, and Lear's representative (Kent/Caius) is treated with scorn. The old patriarchs are pushed aside as Cornwall and Regan exert their authority. The hint that Cordelia will return offers us some hope that the progress of the evil characters might be checked.

GLOSSARY	
14	three-suited servants were given 3 suits a year in service
16	super-serviceable unscrupulous
16	finical fussy, pedantic
19	pander pimp
29	cullionly base, low
72	holy cords the natural bonds of the family
76	halcyon kingfisher. People believed that if you hung a kingfisher up it would twist so that its beak was turned into the wind. The implication here is that fawning, false servants like Oswald will turn their thoughts and deeds to suit their masters
81	Sarum Plain Salisbury Plain
82	Camelot the legendary home of the court of King Arthur

121	**dread** great and heroic (Kent is being sarcastic about Oswald's prowess as a fighter)
123	**Ajax** a self-important and bragging warrior who appears in Homer's Odyssey

SCENE 3

- Edgar disguises himself as the mad beggar, Poor Tom.

Out in the countryside, Edgar is alone. He heard himself proclaimed a criminal, and concealed himself in a tree. His position is desperate; he cannot attempt to flee England as all the ports (seaports and town gates) are watched, and his father's men roam the countryside hunting him down. To preserve his life Edgar decides to disguise himself as a 'Bedlam beggar' (line 14). He describes what he will do to effect this disguise; knot his hair, cover himself in dirt, wear only a blanket for protection.

QUESTION

Discuss the role of disguise and clothing in the play.

COMMENTARY

The audience is left in no doubt as to the difficulties Edgar will face. The fact that he chooses to disguise himself as a social outcast reveals his desperation, and the danger he is in. In Shakespeare's day 'Bedlam' (Bethlehem) hospital housed the mentally ill. When they were released Bedlam inmates were allowed to go begging for survival; this is what Edgar has been reduced to by his brother and father. As in the previous scene, we see goodness pushed aside, degraded and punished. Edgar's situation also mirrors Lear's. Edgar is now reliant on charity, his world and expectations turned upside down. We get a glimpse of what Lear will be reduced to. The contrast between life as absolute monarch and the powerless existence described here could not be more stark. Edgar's assumed madness also points towards Lear's madness in Act III.

GLOSSARY

1	**proclaimed** publicly proclaimed an outlaw
8	**in contempt of** despising, treating with contempt
10	**elf** tangle up into knots
18	**pelting** paltry
19	**bans** curses
20	**Turlygod** there is no really satisfactory explanation for the origins of this word, it is perhaps the name of a beggar

SCENE 4

- Kent is found in the stocks by Lear.
- Lear tries to complain to Regan about Gonerill.
- The sisters reduce his train.
- Angry and distressed, Lear rushes out into the storm.

CONTEXT

Rich householders and European rulers had employed 'all licensed' fools as entertainers for many generations. Fools wore distinctive dress – motley and a coxcomb – and were multi-talented individuals; they sang, danced, performed acrobatics and told witty jokes and riddles. There were female as well as male fools.

Lear arrives at Gloucester's castle, wondering why Regan and Cornwall have not sent Kent/Caius back with a message explaining their movements. The sight of Kent in the stocks upsets him. The Fool mocks Kent while Lear refuses to believe that Cornwall and Regan are responsible for his servant's 'shame' (line 6). Kent recounts his version of the events of the previous day and night. We learn that Cornwall and Regan left home immediately on receipt of Gonerill's letter. A pithy line from the Fool follows Kent's narration. The **image** of wild geese and winter suggests that there is worse to come. The Fool continues to riddle about fathers and their children, but Lear pays him no heed. He is most concerned with his own mental state. Lear fears he is becoming hysterical with sorrow. He demands to know where Regan is and decides to look for her himself. When he leaves the stage Kent asks the Fool why Lear has come with so few followers. He doesn't receive a direct answer, but gets some advice instead: don't follow a master whose power is waning. For all his wisdom on other subjects, the Fool refuses to follow his own advice. He says that he is 'no knave' (line 81) and will stay loyal to Lear.

Lear is angry and incredulous when he returns with Gloucester. Regan and Cornwall have said they are sick and weary and cannot speak with him. Lear thinks that they tricking him. He packs Gloucester off to get a better answer. But even Gloucester thwarts him by trying to excuse Cornwall's behaviour. This enrages Lear further. However, he then accepts that his son-in-law might not be well and decides to be patient. This mood doesn't last long and Lear reverts to his opinion that Cornwall and Regan are deceiving him.

Lear feels himself becoming hysterical once more and tries to control himself. The Fool offers two examples of idiotic kindness. In the first, a cook tries to make an eel pie without killing the eels first because she cannot bear to harm them. In the second, her brother puts butter on his horses' hay to improve the taste.

Cornwall and Regan arrive. Kent is freed. Lear hopes Regan is glad to see him. He is so troubled by this point that he can hardly speak, ending his first speech with a pitiful plea, 'O Regan!' (line 132). However, Regan employs the same sharp tone that Gonerill used so effectively in Act I Scene 4. She tells her father that he should accept his age and failing powers of judgement and be led by others. Her advice is to return to Gonerill and beg her pardon. Lear is astonished. He goes down on his knees, and, in what he thinks is a satirical speech, offers a portrait of himself as a weak old man begging for clothing and shelter. Regan has little patience with these 'unsightly tricks' (line 152) and repeats her instructions. Lear carries on complaining about his eldest daughter. Regan snaps back in an accusatory way; he will curse her too 'when the rash mood is on' (line 164). Lear denies this, saying she is a more natural child. His flattering words have no effect, so Lear shifts his attention back to Kent and asks who put him in the stocks.

At this point Gonerill arrives, disconcerting Lear, who continues to ask how Kent came to be in the stocks. Cornwall smoothly admits that he was responsible for Kent's punishment. Regan's tone becomes harsher; again she tells Lear to go back to Gonerill, and to dismiss half his train. Lear stubbornly continues to refuse this course of action. Gonerill is unconcerned. Lear fears he is losing his wits and curses her. He insists he can stay with Regan and keep his

CHECK THE BOOK
For a discussion of the Fool as wise man, see Gamini Salgado's *King Lear: Text and Performance*, 1984.

knights. Regan contradicts him and then suggests a further reduction in his train. Bewildered, Lear tries to remind his daughters that he gave them everything. They are not impressed. Gradually they argue Lear out of all of his knights.

CHECK THE FILM

My Kingdom (2001), a version of the play set in late twentieth-century Liverpool, updates the story to portray the consequences for family and business when a charismatic, manipulative criminal boss divides his empire among his three daughters.

Agonised, Lear finally bursts out, 'O, reason not the need!' (line 259). He refuses to accept his daughters' way of looking at the world. Man's needs cannot be measured as Gonerill and Regan insist on doing. He points out that even beggars have more than they need. He threatens his daughters that he will be revenged on them. As the storm starts he angrily refuses to weep but then cries out in terror, 'O Fool, I shall go mad!' (line 281). He rushes out.

The sisters justify letting Lear leave because the 'house' (line 283) is too small to accommodate his followers. Gloucester follows Lear out and returns with the news that the king is 'in high rage' (line 291). Gloucester is concerned about Lear's well-being and tells us that the country he has gone out into is desolate, affording little protection from the elements. Clearly, Gloucester would like his guests to call Lear back. But they insist that Lear should be left to suffer the consequences of his actions. Regan instructs Gloucester to lock the doors, still maintaining that the king's followers are dangerous. Lear is left outside in the storm.

COMMENTARY

This scene presents Lear with a number of difficulties, which he finds insurmountable. We watch anxiously as his power and self-possession are stripped away. A number of events and speeches early in the scene point towards the stark outcome, when Lear is rejected by his elder daughters. Kent's presence in the stocks unnerves the king; it is proof that he continues to be treated with contempt, a point reinforced by Cornwall and Regan's refusal to speak with him. Interestingly, Lear seeks Regan out himself instead of sending a servant to fetch her. He is now reduced to conveying his own requests. His powerlessness is emphasised again when his requests for information are ignored; he asks many times how Kent came to be in the stocks before receiving an answer. The pattern of entrances and exits early in the scene mirrors the close of Act I Scene 4, and hints at the chaos to come in Act III. Lear's changes of mood and tone indicate his increasing mental instability. The Fool's disturbing little tales of misguided kindness also operate as a choric introduction (see chorus) to the 'cruel kindness' Gonerill and Regan display later in Act II Scene 1. The perfunctory and frosty greeting between Lear, Cornwall and Regan suggests that Lear is foolish to pin his hopes on his second daughter's kindness. His belief that she would never 'oppose the bolt / Against my coming in' (lines 171–2) is chillingly ironic.

Gonerill's entrance proves to be the turning point for the beleaguered king. Her lack of concern about whether Lear returns to her or not proves that the sisters are oblivious to their father's agitation and suffering. Gonerill and Regan are extremely firm and authoritative when 'measuring out' Lear's knights for him. We are reminded of the dangers of measuring love in words and numbers. Lear's insistence that he will stay with the daughter who allows him to retain the greatest number of followers is as blind and foolish as his 'love-test' in Act I Scene 1. Can he not see that neither of his daughters cares for him? His bargaining is desperate; as impotent as his curses and threats of revenge.

The tone of the speeches that follow Lear's exit is very telling. Gonerill, Regan and Cornwall are unmoved by Lear's agonised final speech; their cool control contrasts starkly with his wild passion. There is a cruel desire to inflict punishment on 'the old man' (line 283) (more contemptuous words). By now the audience will recognise the hypocrisy of Regan's fears about Lear's knights. This scene has proved that Gonerill and Regan are expert manipulators, ready to use any excuse to justify their own actions. When the storm starts, we know that they have 'won'. Lear's fear that he would go mad, first voiced in Act I Scene 4, has been realised.

CONTEXT

Renaissance medical theory was based on theories that were arrived at during the Middle Ages. Shakespeare's contemporaries believed in the imbalance of the four humours; Lear is a choleric man (short-tempered and rash), which might be considered one of the causes of his madness.

GLOSSARY

21	Juno Roman goddess of the Moon
29	a reeking post perspiring messenger
30	Stewed soaked in sweat
34	meiny followers, retine

continued

CONTEXT

Lear's use of the phrase 'Hysterica passio' has been seen by some critics as part of a network of gendered characteristics in the play – father–daughter bonds, the absent Mrs Lear, Lear's own misogyny – in which the feminine is routinely suppressed or denigrated. See essays by McCluskie and Kahn in Kiernan Ryan's *New Casebook* on the play (1993).

55	Hysterica passio a kind of hysteria, which made the afflicted person feel as if they were being suffocated, starting in the womb ('mother'), and then moving up to the heart and throat, hence the idea of 'climbing sorrow'
85	fetches excuses
86	flying off desertion
109	remotion holding themselves aloof, remote from
135	scant neglect, fail to fulfil
159	taking infectious
170	scant my sizes cut down my allowances
211	sumpter pack horse
219	embossed swollen, inflamed

ACT III

SCENE 1

- Out on the heath, Kent and the Gentleman search for Lear.

Kent asks the Gentleman where Lear has gone. We learn that the king is out on the heath, raging against the elements. The Fool is his only companion and he is trying to distract his master with jokes. The Gentleman paints a vivid picture of Lear, tearing his hair, running about unprotected, calling for the destruction of the world. Kent speaks of the recent 'division' between Albany and Cornwall. He goes on to explain that France is preparing to invade England, having already sent some of his army across secretly. Kent gives the Gentleman a ring and asks him to deliver it to Cordelia, who has landed with the French forces at Dover. They continue searching for Lear.

COMMENTARY

Act III occurs in swift short scenes to allow us to see Lear's dramatic descent into madness. We also learn what happens to

Lear's mirror image, Gloucester. There is a spiralling downwards for both characters, culminating in a scene of appalling violence against Gloucester. Lear and Gloucester are both heroic, tragic figures in Act III. Act III Scene 1 sets the scene for us. The Gentleman's descriptions of Lear on the heath prepare us for the sight of the lunatic king in the next scene, and also establish the violence of the storm. Kent provides us with information about another kind of chaos; a clash between the English and French forces. The characters' anxiety about Lear reflects the concern the audience probably feels at this point in the play.

CHECK THE BOOK

For Polish theatre director, Jan Kott, *King Lear* represented the bleakness of the theatre of the absurd: 'of the twelve major characters one half are just and good, the other – unjust and bad. It is a division just as consistent and abstract as in a morality play. But this is a morality play in which everyone will be destroyed: noble characters along with base ones, the persecutors with the persecuted, the torturers with the tortured. Vivisection will go on until the stage is empty.' (*Shakespeare our Contemporary*, 1967)

GLOSSARY

12	**cub-drawn bear** a bear, hungry because she has fed her cubs
12	**couch** shelter
14	**unbonneted** unprotected, without a hat
26	**snuffs and packings** grudges or arguments and secret conspiracies
27	**the hard rein** harsh or cruel treatment
45	**out-wall** outer appearance

SCENE 2

- Increasingly mad, Lear rants in the storm.
- The Fool and Kent try to soothe him.

Out on the heath, Lear rants at the elements. He hopes the tempest will obliterate the world. He wants to see 'ingrateful man' (line 9) destroyed. He ignores the Fool when he pleads with him to return to Gloucester's castle to ask Gonerill and Regan for shelter. Lear then becomes preoccupied with thoughts of his daughters' ingratitude. He offers a heart-rending self-assessment at lines 19–20. Increasingly deranged, he accuses the storm of being in league with Gonerill and Regan. The Fool sings a song and offers an epigram about female vanity and the dangers of promiscuity. Lear won't

CONTEXT

On the Renaissance stage, the sound of thunder was created in one of two ways, either by rolling a bullet on a sheet of metal, or by beating a drum.

engage with the Fool's jibes, willing himself to stay calm and patient ('I will say nothing' – line 38).

Kent catches up with his master, and is concerned by what he sees. His lines are suitably gloomy; he says this storm is so hostile man is unlikely to be able to endure it. Failing to recognise Kent, Lear carries on speaking about what he hopes the storm will uncover. He says that sinners of various kinds should tremble because the gods will find out their crimes. Perhaps he mistakes Kent for one of these sinners when he exclaims 'Tremble, thou wretch' (line 51). Lear concludes that he is 'a man / More sinned against than sinning' (lines 58–9).

Kent spies a hovel nearby, and tries to persuade Lear to take shelter. He intends to return to Gloucester's castle and beg Gonerill and Regan to take their father in. We see a new side of Lear's character when he expresses concern for the Fool and identifies with his suffering. Now he recognises how precious such things as shelter are. Lear asks Kent to lead them to the hovel. Left alone on stage, the Fool makes predictions about Albion's (Britain's) future. Like his master he speaks about the sinners of his own age; dishonest brewers, cutpurses, usurers, pimps and prostitutes. Then he seems to describe a utopia where evil will cease to exist. When criminals turn virtuous – 'that going shall be used with feet' (i.e. things will be as they should – line 94).

> **CONTEXT**
>
> In medieval literature there was a tradition of moral criticism of the rich for their callous treatment of the poor. Lear's criticism of the justice system fits into this tradition. During the same period that *King Lear* was written, Shakespeare also wrote *Measure for Measure*, which questions many ideas about authority and justice.

COMMENTARY

Lear's speeches establish and reflect the properties of the storm. They are full of anger and distress, as the mad king moves swiftly from one topic to another. The violence of the **imagery** Lear employs reflects his state of mind. Lear's isolation is shown by his lack of interaction with the other characters on stage, which also indicates that he is now engaged in an internal struggle; he is battling to preserve his wits. The storm serves as a **metaphor** for Lear – and England's – plight. Lear's obsession with justice and criminal behaviour, introduced in this scene, is maintained until the end of the play. The king has started to consider issues he took too little care of as ruler; his journey towards greater understanding of himself and the world around him has begun.

There are two ways of interpreting the Fool's prophecy. The Fool is either suggesting – optimistically – that virtue will triumph in England, or that optimism about the future is misplaced; even in these terrible days men use their feet for walking. The Fool again provides a moment of relief, a pause in the action where the audience can gather their thoughts.

> **? QUESTION**
>
> Is Lear 'More sinned against than sinning'?

GLOSSARY

2	cataracts	heavy rainstorm
4	thought-executing	as swift as thought
10	court holy-water	flattery
21	servile ministers	willing agents
44	Gallow	scare
50	pudder	chaos, tumult
54	simular of virtue	one who makes a pretence of being virtuous
55	Caitiff	low wretch
58	summoners	a summoner was an official of the church courts
67	scanted	limited, lacking

SCENE 3

- Gloucester tells Edmund he intends to help Lear.
- Edmund decides to betray his father to Cornwall.

The mood is tense as Gloucester frets about the 'unnatural dealing' (line 2) of Cornwall, Regan and Gonerill, who have warned him against helping Lear. Believing that Edmund shares his concern, Gloucester goes on to tell his son that Albany and Cornwall are set to clash and that France has begun his invasion to restore Lear. Gloucester proposes that he and Edmund should assist Lear. He then decides Edmund should act as a decoy, while he goes to find

CONTEXT

Edmund's final couplet in the scene stresses inter-generational rivalry as a key motivator of the play: much as in early modern England where the older generation held power and authority over the young.

the king. When Gloucester leaves, Edmund announces his intention to betray his father to Cornwall.

COMMENTARY

Edmund now has his sights set on his father's title. His decision to betray his father is made without a moment's hesitation, befitting Edmund's ruthless nature. In contrast, Gloucester has prevaricated and shows here that he is anxious about his decision to support Lear. Gloucester's feverish fretting mirrors the alarm the audience will feel at the end of this scene; we know Gloucester is in great danger now. Evil continues to triumph, and good intentions will again be thwarted. Gloucester's earnest desire to assist Lear seems as hopeless and doomed as Kent and the Fool's concern in the previous scene.

GLOSSARY		
12	footed	landed
12	incline to	support, side with
13	privily	secretly

SCENE 4

- Lear continues to rant on the heath.
- Poor Tom is found in a hovel.

Lear, Kent and the Fool reach the hovel. When Kent suggests taking shelter, Lear demurs. He explains that the storm does not affect him because he is suffering inner torment. He says that man only feels bodily complaints when the mind is 'free' (not troubled by worries). He explicitly links the storm with his mental state and returns to the theme that torments him: filial ingratitude. Lear maintains his daughters' cruelty but now seems resigned, 'Pour on; I will endure' (line 18), he says. Again Kent urges Lear to enter the hovel. Lear tells him to take shelter first himself. He seeks isolation and wants to stay out in the storm to pray. In his prayer Lear considers the fate of the homeless.

The Fool rushes out of the hovel, scared by the creature he has found there. Kent kindly takes his hand and calls the 'spirit' out. When Edgar appears as Poor Tom, Lear becomes more demented. Lear instantly recognises himself in Tom, convinced that cruel daughters must have reduced this pitiful specimen to beggary. Poor Tom describes his miserable life, hounded by the 'foul fiend' (line 44). There is a much needed moment of relief when the Fool jokes about Edgar's clothing. The scene becomes more disturbing as Lear asks Poor Tom to recount his history.

Edgar constructs an account of himself as a degenerate servant. It contains references to lechery and the dangers of female sexuality, a theme Lear dwells on in Act IV Scene 6. Tom's presence has a profound effect on Lear. He begins to empathise with the dispossessed and believes that he sees humanity in its essence when he looks at Tom. Lear decides that man is really 'a poor, bare, forked animal' (line 104); he wants to know what it means to have nothing, to be nothing. In his admiration for Tom he tries to undress. Lear wants to remove the superficial trappings that stand between him and 'Unaccommodated man' (line 103). Alarmed, Kent and the Fool try to dissuade Lear from stripping.

During the confusion, Gloucester appears. This is the first time that Edgar has set eyes on his father. Perhaps Edgar fears detection; he seems to behave in a more exaggerated way, chanting and ranting. He sings a song about a female demon who suffocates her victims. As Edgar chants, Kent tries vainly to obtain a response from Lear, who fails to recognise Gloucester. The darkness seems to make the characters nervous. Kent wants to know who Gloucester is and why he has come, and Gloucester asks anxiously about the inhabitants of the hovel. Edgar then launches into an account of seven terrible years as a mad beggar.

Gloucester is dismayed to see the king in such poor company. Tom complains piteously of the cold, but Gloucester ignores him, urging Lear to go with him to a safe place. Lear continues to be most

> **CONTEXT**
>
> Edgar's tales about the 'foul fiend' biting his back reflect Renaissance religious beliefs. People believed in the devil as a palpable presence, who walked abroad, trying to tempt them into evil doing. The devil was also held responsible for ailments in people and animals.

Scene 4 continued

CONTEXT

'Flibberdigibbet' (line 110) is the name of a dancing devil. The names of many of the devils that appear in Act III, and some of the other language that Edgar uses as Poor Tom, are probably taken from a book, *A Declaration of Egregious Popish Impostures* by Samuel Harsnet, which appeared in 1603. In this book Harsnet, who was chaplain to the Bishop of London, wrote scathingly about fraudulent exorcisms carried out by Catholic priests. Edgar's language as Poor Tom reflects the language used by the victims of these exorcisms in Harsnet's book.

concerned with Poor Tom, believing he is a wise Greek philosopher who can teach him. Kent joins Gloucester and pleads with the king to go, but Lear is beyond their help now.

Kent urges Gloucester to leave. Gloucester tells him that Gonerill and Regan seek Lear's death. He also speaks of his own suffering; thoughts of his son's betrayal have sent him half mad with grief. When Gloucester tells Tom to go into the hovel Lear adds 'Come, let's in all' (line 167). He jealously guards the beggar when Kent tries to part them. Kent finally accepts Tom and the characters enter the hovel.

COMMENTARY

This is a scene of isolation and suffering. Each character is oppressed by his own concerns. Kent is agitated because Lear suffers, the Fool shivers in the storm. Both are helpless bystanders. Like Lear, Gloucester is preoccupied by thoughts of filial ingratitude. Edgar's breathless craziness reflects his own sufferings as an outcast and heightens our sense of the king's suffering. His speeches are erratic in a way that Lear's are not, full of terrifying descriptions of physical and mental violence. Through his interaction with Poor Tom, Lear undergoes a terrible kind of purging. In this scene the king also displays the stoicism of a true tragic hero, although his patience seems hard won. His concern for Kent, the Fool and Poor Tom suggests that he is learning compassion, reflected in his lines about the fate of the homeless: 'O, I have ta'en / Too little care of this' (lines 32–3). The pity we feel for Lear increases as he learns to pity others. We also realise that Lear has recognised the need to look beyond appearances when he tries to remove his clothing.

Edgar's description of his life as a corrupt servant can be read as a comment on Oswald's career. Other commentators see Tom's story as a parody of the seven deadly sins. His account of seven years as a beggar seems to be directed at his father, whom he will judge harshly for his adultery later in Act V Scene 3. Lear and Gloucester are both forced to face up to their sins in *King Lear*; Lear has already started to confront his failings.

In spite of the madness and suffering displayed in this scene, some hope remains. The characters sympathise with one another, although Kent is initially reluctant to allow Poor Tom to take shelter with the king. Overall, the prevailing mood is sombre. Poor Tom's references to the 'dark tower' (line 176) and the Jack the giant killer story in the final lines of the scene are ominous. Gloucester's castle now houses four murderous predators (Gonerill, Regan, Cornwall, Edmund) who plot against their fathers.

GLOSSARY

31	**looped and windowed** ragged and full of holes
35	**shake the superflux** give superfluous luxuries or riches to the poor
37	**Fathom and half** the term sailors use to measure the depth of water they are sailing through
53	**halters in his pew** nooses on his balcony
57	**star-blasting** malignant diseases caused by the stars
72	**pelican daughters** a medieval legend. It was believed that young pelicans turned on and killed the parent birds and drank their blood, the implication being that Gonerill and Regan are feeding on and thus killing their father
118	**aroint** get away
126	**sallets** salads
129–30	**three suits to his back, six shirts to his body** the clothing allowance given to the class of servant Edgar is pretending Poor Tom was
136–7	**Smulkin, Modo, Mahu** see context point on p. 38 on Flibberdigibbet. Modo was a name given to Satan, while Mahu was another devil
150	**learnéd Theban** wise Greek scholar

CONTEXT

Some critics have argued that Poor Tom's speeches contain critical comments about the legitimacy of the witchcraft trials that were held in England during the Elizabethan and Jacobean eras. Tom's madness and history of evil-doing as a servant are a sham, while the real criminals, Gonerill and Regan, cause devastation.

SCENE 5

- Edmund betrays Gloucester.

CONTEXT

In the play as printed in 1608 and in 1623, Edmund is routinely called 'Bastard' in speech prefixes and stage directions, perhaps stressing stock associations rather than individual personality.

Cornwall has been given the letter which contains information about the French invasion and intends to punish Gloucester for his treachery. He sends Edmund to find his father. Edmund pretends to be torn between being loyal and to Cornwall and faithful to his 'blood' (line 22), but hopes that he will find his father with Lear. This will make Cornwall even more suspicious. We are left in no doubt as to Cornwall's intentions. He seeks Gloucester's death.

COMMENTARY

The first line of the scene suggests that violence is imminent. This is confirmed by Cornwall's consistently decisive and ruthless tone. Showing his customary facility with language, Edmund speaks politely and formally to Cornwall, who now acts as if he is the father of the nation. Edmund's aside to the audience is as vicious and cold blooded as his new patron's lines. Both evil men lust selfishly and destructively for power.

GLOSSARY

10	**intelligent party to the advantages** spy who is helping advance the French cause
18	**apprehension** arrest

SCENE 6

- Inside the hovel, Lear conducts a trial of Gonerill and Regan.
- Gloucester brings a coach to transport Lear to safety at Dover.

Gloucester and Kent help Lear into the hovel. Gloucester departs, saying he will return with provisions. Poor Tom gibbers about the devil and the Fool continues to taunt Lear with home truths. All the characters seem to be talking to themselves, at cross purposes. Lear is lost in a mad world of his own.

Lear is still preoccupied by thoughts of vengeance. He decides to 'try' his daughters (see **Justice** in **Images and themes** for a discussion of the trials in the play). Lear calls on Poor Tom and the Fool to assist him as justices on the bench. He imagines a joint-stool is Gonerill and accuses 'her' of kicking him. In his madness Lear thinks his eldest daughter has escaped from the 'courtroom' and screams for her to be apprehended. Edgar is in tears as he listens to Lear's lunatic agony. His 'act' momentarily breaks down at 'Bless thy five wits' (line 56). Kent implores Lear to be patient. The king continues with his trial and 'anatomizes' (line 75) Regan. He wants to find out why she has such a hard heart. There is some more black humour, as Lear castigates Poor Tom about his clothes. Kent tries to soothe him again. Finally the old king agrees to rest.

Gloucester returns and says that Lear must be removed to safety immediately because there is a plot to kill him. He has prepared a litter (coach) to transport him to Dover, where he will be met by friends (the French forces).

COMMENTARY

The cold-blooded discussion in Act III. Scene 5 contrasts sharply with the solicitous way Gloucester and Kent continue to behave towards Lear. The mock trial is a parody of the 'love-test' in Act I Scene 1. Here, however, Lear's judgement is not faulty. His madness has helped him to see his daughters clearly. The Fool speaks his last line in the play, 'And I'll go to bed at noon' (line 83). This comically mad remark is an appropriate summing up of this scene. This phrase meant 'to act the fool'. Other commentators feel that the Fool is perhaps referring to a premature death. Again, this is appropriate, and not simply to the Fool. It has now been confirmed that Lear's life is in danger.

CONTEXT

The settings in the play help to convey a sense of disorder; the hovel is the ultimate expression of this. Other settings of chaos include the battlefield, the heath and Dover cliff. These settings are also linked to acts of violence – war, the storm, attempted suicide.

CONTEXT

The mock trial in the hovel was omitted from the Folio (final) version of the play. There have been many suggestions as to why the scene was cut. Many feel the scene is 'unactable', so Shakespeare removed it.

GLOSSARY

2	piece out add to
6	Fraterretto another dancing devil from Harsnet
6	Nero a corrupt, lascivious Roman emperor, reputedly insane
25	Bessy the subject of a popular song at the time
30	Hoppedance another dancing devil from Harsnet
37	yokefellow of equity partner in law
43	minikin either shrill or attractive, sweet
68	lym bloodhound
69	trundle-tail curly tailed dog
74	thy horn is dry Bedlam beggars used horns for begging drinks. The suggestion here is that Edgar is 'worn out', empty. He is exhausted by playing the part of Poor Tom and by observing Lear's distressing madness
104	o'erskip avoid
109	high noises reports of goings on amongst the important people
109	bewray uncover, reveal oneself
113	Lurk, lurk stay concealed, in hiding

SCENE 7

- Cornwall and Regan take out their horrible revenge on Gloucester.

Cornwall tells Gonerill to return to Albany and show him Gloucester's letter (containing the news of the French invasion). He expects Albany to join forces with him. Cornwall then tells his servants to seek out Gloucester. Regan says Gloucester should be hanged immediately, while Gonerill prefers a more vicious form of torture – the plucking out of his eyes. Edmund is sent to accompany Gonerill on her journey home. We know Gloucester will suffer horribly when Cornwall says to Edmund, 'the revenges we are bound to take upon your traitorous father are not fit for your beholding' (lines 7–9). Cornwall calls Edmund 'My lord of Gloucester' (line 14), sealing the old earl's fate. Gloucester is not expected to survive his punishment. Oswald brings news that Gloucester has helped Lear escape to Dover with thirty-five or six of his loyal knights. In a reversal of the way justice should work, Cornwall proposes to pass sentence on Gloucester without trial.

Gloucester is brought in. He knows that his guests mean to harm him. Regan speaks to him venomously, and disrespectfully plucks him by the beard – a foretaste of the violence to come. Gloucester is tied to a chair, and asks fearfully, 'What will you do?' (line 41). He compares himself to a bear in the sport of bear-baiting; he is tied to a stake while the dogs savage him. He must endure. He says that he sent Lear to Dover because he could not bear to see him tortured by Gonerill and Regan. Gloucester also describes Lear's sufferings out in the 'hell-black night' (line 59) of the storm. When Gloucester says he hopes to see 'The wingèd Vengeance overtake such children' (line 65), Cornwall gouges out one of Gloucester's eyes. Regan urges her husband to pluck out his other eye.

CHECK THE BOOK

For a discussion of the characters of evil in the play, see Gamini Salgado's *King Lear: Text and Performance*, 1984.

One of Cornwall's servants steps in. Appalled by what he sees, he bids Cornwall stop. The two men draw their swords and fight and Cornwall is wounded. Regan takes a sword from another servant and runs the challenger through. In spite of his wound, Cornwall finds the strength to put out Gloucester's other eye, mocking his victim. Gloucester hopes that Edmund will revenge him. Regan taunts Gloucester, informing the old man that Edmund hates his father. Gloucester recognises that he has been deceived and calls on the gods to protect Edgar and forgive him for doubting his true son. Regan tells servants to 'thrust' Gloucester 'out at gates and let him smell / His way to Dover' (lines 92–3). She then helps her wounded husband from the stage. Two servants decide to help Gloucester and fetch some medicine to soothe his wounded eyes. They want to take him to Poor Tom, who can act as his guide.

COMMENTARY

This scene contains one of the most shocking acts of physical violence in any of Shakespeare's plays. The physical torture here matches the mental agony Lear has endured in Act III. There are

QUESTION

How does the Gloucester subplot add to your understanding of the play?

many references to eyes and sight that increase the tension we feel and prepare us for Gloucester's blinding, beginning with Gonerill's 'Pluck out his eyes' (line 5). Even though she does not take part in Gloucester's maiming, her suggestion implicates Gonerill in this crime. Like Lear, Gloucester achieves heroism through suffering. Like Kent, he suffers because he has tried to help Lear. In this scene, which contains some of his most powerful speeches in the play, Gloucester is eloquent, brave and determined as he defends himself and castigates Cornwall and Regan for their cruelty to the king. The Earl becomes the voice of the audience, describing their outrage. Like Lear, Gloucester learns the truth about his children in a particularly brutal way. He also shares Lear's agony when he discovers that he has been taken in by outward appearances. The barbarism of the whole scene is summed up by Regan's final callous order to the servants.

The cruelty of this scene indicates that the world has been turned upside down in *King Lear*. A woman suggests a method of torture, another woman relishes inflicting pain, egging her husband on to further cruelty before killing a man herself. There is another miscarriage of justice. A servant turns on his master. This act of heroism prepares us for the kindness the servants show Gloucester at the end of the scene. Although the play has reached its lowest point before the tragic final scene, the generous actions of the servants in Act III Scene 7 indicate that there is some kind of justice at work.

GLOSSARY		
10	festinate	swift
16	Hot questrists	followers, who are seeking Lear urgently
39	quicken	bind by the arms
57	anointed flesh	this is a reference to Lear's status as God's deputy on earth, who rules by divine right (a Christian idea which is at odds with the pagan setting of the play). At the coronation monarchs were anointed with holy oil, reconfirming their sacred status
62	dern	awful, dreadful

> **64**   **All cruels else subscribe** there are different interpretations of this line. It might mean that Gonerill and Regan would have allowed any cruel or wild beast into the castle on such a stormy night, but not Lear (emphasising their cruelty). Or perhaps the line suggests that on this terrible night any other cruel creature would have pitied Lear and given him shelter, but not his barbaric daughters

ACT IV

SCENE 1

- Edgar comes across his blind, suicidal father and starts to lead him to Dover.

Edgar considers the merits of being a poor, despised outcast. At least a beggar has nothing to lose or fear – he cannot sink any lower. Gloucester is led on by an old man, and Edgar's fragile optimism is shattered.

Gloucester suffers deeply. He tells the old man to leave, concerned that he will be punished for helping him. Gloucester says he has lost his way in life and wishes to 'see' Edgar again, so that he can ask for his forgiveness. This moves Edgar, whose lines reflect the despair his father feels. Gloucester offers a dark view of the world and those who rule man's fate, 'As flies to wanton boys are we to the gods; / They kill us for their sport' (lines 36–7).

The old man calls to Edgar/ Poor Tom to assist Gloucester. Edgar is torn between continuing in his disguise and revealing his identity. Gloucester begs the old man to fetch some clothes for Poor Tom. The old man is doubtful about leaving Gloucester alone with Tom, but Gloucester says that it is appropriate for a lunatic to lead a blind man. He asks Tom to lead him to Dover, and gives him money for his services. Edgar is still distressed and has difficulty in maintaining his disguise.

CHECK THE FILM

Brook's 1970 film sets the scene of Gloucester's blinding amid butchery implements and hanging joints of meat. At the moment when Cornwall leans forward to gouge out Gloucester's eye, the frame goes black, giving a strong sense that we are seeing the scene from his perspective and hearing his agonised screams.

Like Lear, Gloucester is preoccupied by thoughts of justice. He hopes the rich man, who has too much and 'will not see / Because he does not feel' (lines 67–8), will have his eyes opened by the gods. He suggests that man needs to be stripped of his excess wealth in order to see clearly. He says that wealth should be distributed more evenly so that 'each man have enough' (line 70). Gloucester's final speech conveys his desire to die. He promises Edgar further financial reward if he leads him 'to the very brim' (line 74) of the cliff. We understand that he intends to attempt suicide.

COMMENTARY

CHECK THE BOOK

For a discussion of power and morality in the play, see Kiernan Ryan, *Shakespeare: Texts and Contexts*, 2000.

At the start of the scene Edgar seems to feel positive; his experiences have taught him to withstand the 'blasts' (line 9) of Fortune. Like Gloucester and Lear, he is learning to endure. Gloucester's stoicism is severely tested in Act IV Scene 1. His view of the sadistic gods shows us clearly that he has been pushed to the limits of endurance. Are we to accept Gloucester's verdict as an accurate description of the world of *King Lear*? Or is his pessimism a reflection of his current state of mind? At his most desolate, Gloucester acts generously towards others, speaking graciously to the old man and Poor Tom. He seems more concerned with their fortunes than his own. If the gods are cruel, this scene proves again that man can be kind. Gloucester's interest in social justice reflects Lear's, and proves that the patriarchs have learned to see the world clearly. As Gloucester says so aptly; he 'stumbled' (line 19) when he saw. For Gloucester, clarity of vision brings despair. Edgar's role in this scene is to guide our responses to his father's misery.

GLOSSARY	
11	mutations changes
51	daub cover up, pretend
58	Obdicut, Hobbididence more demons, probably from Harsnet
67	ordinance will or divine rule

SCENE 2

- Gonerill and Edmund return to Gonerill's residence.
- Albany accuses Gonerill of cruelty to her father. He also learns of the blinding of Gloucester.

Gonerill and Edmund have returned from Gloucester's castle. Gonerill is surprised that her husband has not come out to greet them. Oswald tells her that Albany has undergone a radical change of heart. He is glad of the French invasion and appalled by Edmund's treachery to his father. Gonerill says her husband is a coward. She tells Edmund to return to Cornwall to help with the preparations for battle. Gonerill offers herself to Edmund. She says that she will shortly command him as his mistress. Edmund pledges his loyalty to her.

Albany appears and Gonerill greets him sarcastically. In return, Albany is eloquent in his denigration of Gonerill. She is a devil. The sisters have behaved like 'Tigers not daughters' (line 40). Gonerill coolly disregards these insults. Albany's language becomes more violent as he describes how he would like to tear Gonerill limb from limb. A messenger arrives with the news that Cornwall has died. Albany says this is just and shows sympathy for Gloucester. The messenger also has a letter for Gonerill, from Regan. Gonerill is suspicious of her sister. She is concerned that Regan will seek to marry Edmund. The sisters are now rivals for Edmund's love. In spite of her concerns, Gonerill does not seem unduly alarmed. She leaves to read and answer Regan's letter.

Albany is still thinking about Gloucester. He asks the messenger where Edmund was when Gloucester was tortured. On learning the truth he resolves to revenge Gloucester and support Lear's cause.

COMMENTARY

The change in Albany suggests that the influence of the evil characters will no longer go unchecked. Albany becomes a figure of justice and morality in this scene, voicing the audience's concerns

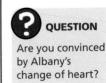

QUESTION

Are you convinced by Albany's change of heart?

about his wife. Gonerill continues to assume authority, disregarding her husband and wooing Edmund. Her desires and actions are subversive and immoral. We are presented with a clash between good (Albany) and evil (Gonerill), which points towards the battle between the French and British forces at the end of Act IV.

GLOSSARY		
16	musters	calling together or recruiting troops of soldiers
16	conduct	lead, head
17	distaff	the stick used to spin wool (a female pursuit. Gonerill implies she's more a man than her husband: he is fit only for woman's work)
42	head-lugged	a bear pulled along by its head
62	self-covered	disguised
87	tart	bitter (in the sense of bad tasting)

CHECK THE FILM
Peter Brook's black and white film (1970) cuts Cordelia's asides in Act I Scene 1 before she speaks of her love, thus denying us a point of sympathy with her. This decision is of a piece with the bleak mood of this production, with an emotional chill emphasised by the exterior snowscapes.

SCENE 3

- Kent and the Gentleman speak of Cordelia, and how Lear is too ashamed to see her.

Kent asks a Gentleman why the King of France has returned home. We learn that he had urgent state business to attend to. Kent asks the Gentleman how Cordelia reacted when she read his letters (describing Lear's treatment at the hands of Gonerill and Regan). We are told that 'holy water' fell from her 'heavenly eyes' (line 30) as she lamented Lear's plight. Kent reports Lear's arrival in Dover. The king is now sometimes 'in his better tune' (line 39) but so ashamed of his 'unkindness' (line 42) to Cordelia that he will not see her. The Gentleman says that Albany and Cornwall's forces are 'afoot' (line 49). Kent takes him to attend on Lear.

COMMENTARY

This scene prepares us for Cordelia's return. Lear's youngest daughter is now the epitome of graceful, Christian femininity, described as compassionate and loving. We know that the reconciliation between Lear and Cordelia will be painful and poignant. Lear has started to regain his wits, but clarity of vision brings with it distress and regret. Father and daughter now share the same emotion: sorrow.

GLOSSARY

31	clamour, moistened	there are two possible meanings: either that Cordelia is so overcome her speech is stopped by her tears, or that she was crying while she spoke
39	better tune	in his right mind
44	casualties	chances (Cordelia was left to take her chance abroad in France when Lear rejected her)
49	afoot	marching on their way

SCENE 4

- Cordelia sends her soldiers to search for Lear, who is still wandering around outside.
- She expresses deep concern for her father.

Cordelia describes how Lear has been seen, mad and singing, wearing a crown of flowers and weeds. She sends one hundred soldiers out to find Lear and calls on the earth to help restore him. A messenger informs her that the British army is drawing closer. To allay any fears the audience might have of a foreign invasion, Cordelia insists that she has come to defend Lear's rights; she is motivated by love, not political ambition. She hopes fervently that she will soon see and hear Lear.

COMMENTARY

Lear's crown of weeds has symbolic significance. The king is now associated with nature rather than the world of the court, which is fitting given his interest in justice and the human condition. In keeping with the descriptions of her in the previous scene, Cordelia

CONTEXT

Readings of Cordelia's character which suggest she is a Christ-like figure rest on her lines which suggest she has her father's interests at heart. Her words echo Christ's in Luke 2: 49, 'O dear father, it is thy business I go about'.

shows great compassion for her father. He is her sole concern. Like Edgar, she actively assists the parent who rejected her so cruelly.

GLOSSARY

3	**fumiter** fumitory (a weed)
3	**furrow-weeds** the weeds that grow in fields that have been ploughed. All the weeds Lear is wearing are poisonous or bitter tasting. Weeds are also destructive. They are appropriate to his current state
26	**importuned** appears as 'important' in the Quarto, beseeching

---

SCENE 5

- Regan interrogates Oswald about a letter he is carrying from Gonerill to Edmund.

Regan asks Oswald why Gonerill has written to Edmund. She tries to persuade him to show her the letter he is carrying. She tells Oswald that Edmund has ridden away to finish off Gloucester and find out how strong the French forces are. Regan also admits that it was a mistake to let Gloucester live: people who have heard of his cruel treatment have turned against her. She tries to prevent Oswald's departure, saying 'the ways are dangerous' (line 17). However, Oswald is as diligent as ever and insists that he must go. Regan asks again to see the letter and then adopts a threatening tone. She and Edmund have talked, and agreed on marriage. Gonerill must be warned off. Regan gives Oswald a letter or gift for Edmund and asks him to deliver it. She casually mentions the fact that there is a reward for anyone who kills Gloucester.

COMMENTARY

Regan's preoccupation with her own selfish lust contrasts sharply with Cordelia's generosity in the previous scene. Throughout Act IV, Lear's daughters are juxtaposed, scene by scene. We watch the

CHECK THE BOOK

For a discussion of the theme of service and self-promotion in the play, see John Russell Brown, *Shakespeare: The Tragedies*, 2001.

progress of both good and evil. The language Regan uses to describe her liaison with Edmund is entirely in keeping with the materialistic desires of the evil characters; Edmund is 'more convenient' (line 31) for her than Gonerill. It seems that Gonerill and Regan are now divided by their rivalry in love, while the good characters share the same aims and appear to be gathering strength. The fact that people are appalled by Gloucester's blinding suggests that we might be justified in hoping that evil might be vanquished.

GLOSSARY		
13	nighted	darkened
13	descry	discover, find out
25	oeillades	loving looks

SCENE 6

- Gloucester tries to commit suicide at Dover.
- Lear and Gloucester meet for the last time.
- Edgar saves Gloucester's life when Oswald threatens him.

Edgar leads Gloucester to Dover. He pretends they are labouring up a steep hill to the cliff top and asks Gloucester if he can hear the sea. Gloucester's other senses are more acute now that he is blind; he thinks he is walking on even ground and has also noticed that Edgar speaks differently. Edgar dismisses these ideas. He describes the view from the cliff top. Pretending to feel dizzy, Edgar says they are so high up it is impossible to hear the sea. Gloucester asks to be moved to the edge of the cliff. He gives his peasant guide a jewel as payment for his services. Edgar informs us that he has deceived Gloucester in order to 'cure' (line 34) his despair. Kneeling, Gloucester announces to the gods that he intends to kill himself. The pain he feels is too much for him. His final generous thoughts are of his son Edgar and the beggar who has helped him. There follows the extraordinary sight of Gloucester throwing himself off the imaginary cliff and falling on the ground. Edgar worries that

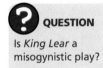

QUESTION

Is *King Lear* a misogynistic play?

Gloucester's desire to kill himself might actually have caused his death.

When Gloucester revives he is still suicidal. Pretending to be a passerby on the beach, Edgar now tries to chase away his father's gloomy thoughts. He tells him his life must have been preserved by a miracle. Gloucester is wretched when he hears Edgar's description of his 'fall'; he has been unable to find comfort in death and feels the gods have thwarted him. Edgar persists. He urges Gloucester to stand and helps him up. He describes the strange creature on the cliff top, implying that a devil drove his father to attempt suicide. Edgar tries desperately to convince his father that the kind gods have saved him. This explanation seems to forge a change of heart in Gloucester, who now declares that he will endure life until life itself gives up on him.

Lear enters, wearing his crown of weeds. Edgar is appalled to see that his mind is still ravaged. Lear speaks in a disjointed way, about money, justice and archery. He insists that he is 'the King himself' (line 84) and declares he will defend himself against anyone, even a giant. Gloucester recognises Lear's voice and a strange, cruel exchange ensues. Lear mistakes Gloucester for Gonerill 'with a white beard' (line 96) and launches into a tirade against female sexuality. Lear's fear of monstrous femininity also leads him to introduce the topic of Gloucester's adultery. Perhaps one part of his fevered brain recognises his old friend. There is a cruel irony in Lear's lines about Gloucester's 'kind' bastard son. The cruelty continues as Lear seems to mock the old Earl's blindness, talking about blind Cupid and asking Gloucester to read a summons he has drawn up. Gloucester responds to Lear with pity and reverence. As Lear taunts him he begs to be allowed to kiss the king's hand.

Lear is obsessed with social and moral justice. He talks about how thieves are condemned by corrupt justices of the peace. But with a bribe the justice will let the thief off, so who is the real thief? Authority is a sham: even a dog is obeyed in office because of his status. Lear then seems to see hypocrites appearing before him; a beadle who whips a prostitute but lusts after her himself, a money lender who hangs a petty cheat. Lear disparages rich sinners who are able to break the 'strong lance of justice' (line 167), while beggars cannot escape punishment for their crimes because they have no money to make bribes. Lear seems to have reached radical conclusions about human justice. He wants to defend the poor and give them power.

Lear offers Gloucester something to 'seal th'accuser's lips' (line 171). Perhaps he wants Gloucester to bribe a justice to look leniently on one of the poor sinners he has described. He then advises Gloucester to get glasses so that he can act like a cunning politician, who conjures up intrigues to justify his actions. Lear asks Gloucester to pull off his boots. He acknowledges his friend in two lines of perfect sense, telling him to be patient. Lear then offers a pessimistic assessment of the human condition: it is man's lot to suffer and endure.

At this point Cordelia's attendants arrive. Lear seems to see them as hostile figures and runs off. The attendants pursue him while the Gentleman remains behind. Edgar asks him for news of the battle that is expected between the French and British forces. Gloucester's encounter with Lear seems to have driven away thoughts of suicide. Lear's appalling condition has made him realise that his own suffering is not so unendurable. Edgar says he will lead Gloucester to a safe place.

As they prepare to leave, Oswald comes upon Edgar and Gloucester. He is delighted because he will now be able to claim Regan's reward. Gloucester welcomes Oswald's sword. Assuming the accent of a country bumpkin, Edgar challenges Oswald, who is fatally wounded in the fight. In his dying speech Oswald asks Edgar to take the letters he is carrying to Edmund. Regretting that he had to act as Oswald's 'deathsman' (line 258), Edgar sums up the self-seeking servant neatly as the corrupt follower of an evil mistress. He reads the letters and discovers Gonerill's plot against Albany's life. Shocked, he decides to inform Albany of the contents of the letter when the time is right. He drags Oswald's body offstage for burial. Meanwhile Gloucester is preoccupied by thoughts of Lear's lunacy. He wishes he could be mad like Lear, believing that madness would distract him from his agony. In spite of the stoicism he has shown in

> **CONTEXT**
>
> Oswald was the name of the first Christian king of Northumberland, later Saint Oswald. Is Shakespeare's use of the name therefore perhaps ironic?

Act IV, Gloucester finds it very difficult to maintain cheerful thoughts. Edgar returns to escort his father to safety at the French camp. A drum roll suggests the battle is imminent.

COMMENTARY

Edgar's description of the view from the cliff top serves two purposes; to convince his father that he stands on the edge of the cliff and to show Gloucester's desperation. His **aside** at line 42 hints at the terror created by Gloucester's attempted suicide, which can seem both tragic and absurd in performance. As previously, he guides our responses to Gloucester. Edgar says very little when Lear is on stage, offering brief asides. His words emphasise the **pathos** of the exchange between Lear and Gloucester. Both patriarchs seem worn out, but they 'see how this world goes' (lines 148–9) now. They have achieved understanding and wisdom through suffering. Lear's lines about adultery might be read as an attempt to come to terms with his own sexual union with his daughters' mother – did he cause those hard hearts? Lear also seems to be playing the same role for Gloucester that the Fool played for him. He is a cruel commentator in this scene. His obsession with justice fits in with his earlier concern for 'unaccommodated man' (III.4.103).

At the end of the scene Edgar takes on a more active role when he defends his father. He will play the role of revenger again in Act V Scene 3. His energetic goodness offers us hope. It seems that Gloucester and Lear's pessimism about the human condition is not entirely justified.

GLOSSARY

13	**choughs** crows
15	**sampire** samphire, a plant that grows on cliffs, used by Elizabethans as a vegetable and in pickles
71	**welked** twisted
87	**press-money** the money paid to new recruits, who had probably been press-ganged into the army
91	**I' the clout** on target

93	**Sweet marjoram** a herb that was used for treating diseases of the brain
119	**forks** legs
122	**fitchew** polecat (also a slang term for a prostitute)
124	**centaurs** a mythical creature, half man, half horse, which had a reputation for lust
130	**civet** a strong musky perfume
161	**beadle** a parish constable
241	**costard** apple (meaning Oswald's head here)
241	**ballow** stick, cudgel
245	**foins** the thrusts of Oswald's weapon

SCENE 7

- Cordelia and Lear are reunited and reconciled.

Lear has been brought to the French camp near Dover. Cordelia thanks Kent for his services. Modest as ever, Kent says he does not need repayment. Cordelia urges him to put aside his disguise but he says he still needs it. We learn that Lear is asleep. Cordelia prays to 'the kind gods' (line 14) to restore her father's senses. The Doctor says it is time to wake Lear, who has been dressed in fresh garments while sleeping. The old king is carried on in a chair and all the characters on stage prostrate themselves before him. The Doctor calls for music. Before Lear wakes Cordelia kneels by his chair, hoping that her kiss will make up for some of the 'violent harms' (line 28) done by her sisters.

Lear wakes up. He is bewildered and thinks he is in hell, 'bound / Upon a wheel of fire' (lines 47–8). He does not seem to recognise his daughter, who asks for his blessing. Lear falls on his knees before her, showing that he regrets wronging Cordelia. He sees himself clearly as 'a very foolish fond old man' (line 60). Cordelia denies that she has any reason to feel bitter towards her father. She

CONTEXT

The powerful healing properties of music are shown in a number of Shakespeare's plays, including the late Romance, *The Winter's Tale*.

 QUESTION

Do you agree that Lear loses the world and gains his soul?

asks Lear if he would like to walk with her. Father and daughter leave the stage together. Kent and the Gentleman remain behind to discuss the battle. Edmund has been put in charge of Cornwall's men. A bloody confrontation is expected.

COMMENTARY

This is a scene of **pathos** and renewal. Sleep and music were understood to have powerful healing properties. Our sense of restoration is heightened when the characters kneel before Lear, who is treated as a powerful monarch. All the words addressed to him are respectful and he sits 'above' his subjects once more. However, we quickly realise that Lear is not the towering figure he once was. His speeches are hesitant, and he humbles himself before Cordelia. He no longer speaks of himself as the royal 'we'. Lear understands that he sinned against his youngest daughter and wishes to honour her. He does not accept responsibility for Gonerill and Regan, however. They are now identified (in Cordelia's lines before Lear awakes) as the sole cause of the king's suffering. We are expected to view Lear as a victim now.

Certainly, this is the view Lear holds himself. His lines are full of self-pity. This scene comes as an immense relief after the chaos and darkness of Acts III and IV, although news of the battle suggests the harmony that is achieved here is already under threat.

CHECK THE BOOK

For a discussion of Lear's relationship with Cordelia, see John Russell Brown, *Shakespeare: The Tragedies*, 2001.

CONTEXT

Many would argue that the tragedy of this play is that wisdom comes too late.

GLOSSARY		
7	weeds	clothes
35	perdu	lost one
94	arbitrament	outcome of the battle

ACT V

SCENE 1

- Regan questions Edmund about his feelings for Gonerill.
- Edgar gives Albany the letter disclosing Edmund and Gonerill's plot against his life.
- Edmund says he will show Lear and Cordelia no mercy after the battle.

Act V opens with preparations for the clash between the British and French armies. Edmund begins decisively, complaining to Regan that Albany keeps changing his plans. Regan fears that something has happened to Oswald. She asks Edmund if he loves Gonerill. Albany and Gonerill arrive with Albany's forces. Seeing Regan and Edmund together, Gonerill says she would rather lose the battle than Edmund. Albany speaks sympathetically about the reasons for the French invasion but Gonerill insists that they must all unite against the enemy now. Albany agrees and says that they must consult 'th'ancient of war' (experienced campaigners – line 32) about the best way to proceed in battle. Edmund agrees to discuss strategy in Albany's tent. Regan asks Gonerill to accompany them. She refuses. Gonerill realises Regan is concerned about leaving her alone with Edmund. But then she changes her mind and goes with the others. As Albany makes to leave, Edgar (still disguised) appears and asks to speak with him. He gives Albany the letter he found on Oswald and tells him to open it before going into battle. He asks Albany to have a trumpet sounded if Britain wins the battle, so that a champion may appear to prove the truth of the contents of the letter.

Edmund returns with the news that the French are approaching. Left alone on stage he muses about his predicament. He has sworn his love to both Gonerill and Regan, and cannot decide which one to 'take' (line 57). He knows the sisters are so jealous that one will have to die in order for him to 'enjoy' the other. Edmund decides to wait and see what happens in the battle. He informs us that Albany

QUESTION

Edmund has been described as the 'wittiest and most attractive of villains'. Do you agree with this assessment?

intends to show mercy to Lear and Cordelia if the British win. But Edmund has other plans for them. They must die.

COMMENTARY

This is a scene of uneasiness and some urgency. Gonerill and Regan's feud over Edmund continues, Gonerill and Albany are at odds, and Albany and Edmund clearly share different intentions about the battle and its outcome. Edmund's brief responses to Regan suggest his impatience or discomfort with love talk. In his first **soliloquy** he reveals his callous approach to matrimony, which matches the ruthlessness he has shown in all his dealings with others in *King Lear*. His only loyalty is to himself. His last three lines suggest that Edmund revels in his newly exalted position and power. We fear the outcome of the battle and wonder how the rivalry between Gonerill and Regan will be resolved.

GLOSSARY		
11	forfended	forbidden
12	conjunct	intimate with
13	bosomed with	embraced by
30	broils	arguments, quarrel

SCENE 2

www. CHECK THE NET
www.net explosure.com/ **Kinglear**: the full text of the play can be found here, together with famous quotations, images and a basic self-test quiz on the play.

- The French forces are defeated in battle.
- Edgar leads Gloucester to safety for the last time.

Cordelia, Lear and the French forces march across the stage, and Edgar leads Gloucester on, bringing him to a safe place while the battle rages. He leaves briefly and then returns with the news that the French have lost. Lear and Cordelia have been captured. Overcome by pessimistic thoughts, Gloucester refuses to leave with Edgar, who chides him. He implies that man should not sit and 'rot' as Gloucester says he wishes to. He must prepare himself for death and await the moment chosen for him. Gloucester allows himself to be led away.

COMMENTARY

The battle is dealt with perfunctorily. Shakespeare is most interested in its consequences. We get an indication of what is to occur in the final scene when Edgar says, 'Men must endure / Their going hence even as their coming hither;/ Ripeness is all' (lines 9–11). Gloucester still wishes to die, and we know that Lear (now a prisoner) is in great danger. Both old men have endured more than enough. The tragic stoicism of these lines prepares us for the outcome of Act V Scene 3.

GLOSSARY

11	Ripeness readiness

SCENE 3

- Lear and Cordelia are sent away to prison. Edmund sends a death warrant after them.
- Albany accuses Gonerill and Edmund of treason and Edgar appears to challenge Edmund.
- Edmund is fatally wounded in the fight. Gonerill poisons Regan, and stabs herself.
- Lear carries in the dead body of Cordelia and dies, mourning her.

CONTEXT

There are many examples of revengers in Renaissance drama. Many are dubious figures, but Edgar is a benign revenger, an upright figure who is driven to set things right.

Signalling the triumph of evil, Edmund leads on his prisoners to the sound of drums. He orders officers to take Lear and Cordelia away. Cordelia expresses her dismay at being captured, but couches it in terms of compassion for Lear. She asks Edmund whether she and Lear will see Gonerill and Regan. Lear is horrified; he cannot bear the idea of setting eyes on his eldest daughters again. Instead he says he would be pleased to go to prison with Cordelia. He imagines imprisonment as a time of happiness away from the superficial cares of the court. He embraces Cordelia protectively. She is his only concern, as he is hers. Cordelia is crying. Lear tells her to wipe away her tears, and offers a defiant view of his new bond with his daughter.

Lear and Cordelia are escorted to prison. Edmund orders a captain to follow them and gives him a death warrant. It seems that Edmund is now aiming at the crown. However, he has underestimated Albany, who now enters with Gonerill, Regan and officers. After briefly praising Edmund's courage in battle, Albany demands to see the prisoners. Edmund hedges. Lear and Cordelia will be ready to appear for judgement in two or three days. For once, his eloquence fails him. Albany interrupts icily with a rebuke, telling Edmund he is his subject, not his 'brother' (equal) and should be ruled by him. This annoys Regan, who defends Edmund. The sisters start to squabble. Gonerill says Edmund's personal merits 'exalt' (line 68) him; he doesn't need any title Regan can confer on him to make him worthy. Regan announces her intention of marrying Edmund. Albany insults Edmund as 'Half-blooded' (line 81) and arrests him for treason.

Albany then sounds the trumpet to call Edmund's accuser. He announces his own willingness to challenge Edmund. We now learn that Gonerill has poisoned Regan, who complains of feeling increasingly unwell. Edmund remains defiant. He declares his intention to 'maintain / My truth and honour firmly' (lines 101–2). Regan is carried away sick. On the third trumpet Edgar appears, armed. He accuses Edmund of betraying Albany, 'thy gods, thy brother, and thy father' (line 132). Edmund is impressed by Edgar's 'fair and warlike' (line 140) exterior, and agrees to fight. He is wounded. Dismayed, Gonerill says the fight was unlawful. Albany confronts her with her letter to Edmund. Gonerill tries to tear it up; like her paramour, she is defiant to the last. She tries a last desperate attempt at asserting her power before running off.

As he lies dying, Edmund confesses his crimes. He says he will forgive his adversary if he is a nobleman. Edgar puts aside his

CONTEXT

Some critics feel that the final scene ends on a faintly optimistic note. Edgar was the name of a king who united England and Scotland; so if Gloucester's son is now in charge, perhaps reunification of Lear's battered kingdom is possible.

disguise. He judges Edmund and his father harshly. Edmund admits the justice of Edgar's remarks and stoically accepts his own death. Albany embraces Edgar. Edgar then recounts his own history since the play began, including his attempts to keep Gloucester from despair. He regrets remaining in disguise so long. He is particularly distressed when he describes Gloucester's death. It seems that his reunion with Edgar was too much for Gloucester, whose heart, ''Twixt two extremes of passion, joy and grief, / Burst smilingly' (lines 196–7). Albany is overwhelmed by this tale of woe, but Edmund says it has moved him, 'and shall perchance do good' (line 198).

The final movement of the play begins when the Gentleman enters carrying a bloody knife. Gonerill has killed herself and Regan too is dead. Kent comes to 'bid my King and master aye good night' (line 233). Kent's words bring Albany to a stark realisation – he has forgotten all about Lear. He urgently asks Edmund where he sent Lear and Cordelia. Gonerill and Regan's bodies are dragged on to the stage. A moment of panic ensues as Albany and Edmund try to establish how to repeal the death warrant, but it is much too late.

As Edmund is carried off to die, Lear comes in with Cordelia's body in his arms. He is distraught and asks for a feather to place on Cordelia's lips. He hopes that his daughter still breathes. Kent asks in horror, 'Is this the promised end?' (line 261). Lear calls all those around him murderers and traitors for allowing Cordelia to die. We learn that he committed one last act of heroism in his daughter's defence: he killed her hangman. Lear then seems to tumble into madness again; his eyesight fails him, all his senses give up the fight to live. Kent tells Lear of Gonerill and Regan's deaths, but this has no effect on the grieving man. A messenger brings news that Edmund has died.

Albany says that he intends resigning his power to Lear. He also says that Edgar and Kent will receive back their rights as earls, and be rewarded with new honours. Lear continues to grieve over Cordelia's corpse. Choking, he asks someone to undo his button. Edgar rushes to his aid but Kent tells him to let be; Lear will welcome death after the sufferings of his life. Sorrowfully, he adds that he too expects to die soon. He brushes off Albany's suggestions

QUESTION

In what ways do you find the final scene an effective ending to a tragedy?

CONTEXT

The last lines of the play are attributed differently in the Quarto and Folio versions of the text. In the Quarto (the earlier version of the play), Albany speaks the final lines. In the Folio, the same lines are given to Edgar. Usually, in Shakespeare's plays, the highest ranking surviving figure speaks the closing lines. So, if Edgar speaks the lines, there is a definite sense that there has been a shift in power.

about sharing power and ruling Britain. Lear dies, perhaps believing that Cordelia still lives. Albany and Edgar are left to sustain the 'gored' (line 318) state. Edgar calls on everyone to speak plainly and honestly and acknowledge their grief. He also says the survivors 'Shall never see so much nor live so long' (line 324), suggesting that lives of those who remain have been shattered by the events of Act V Scene 3.

COMMENTARY

Events occur swiftly in this tragic final scene, which is dominated by violent deaths. There is a brief moment of hope when Lear describes his life with Cordelia in prison, but his dreams are revealed as an illusion almost immediately. Thereafter, sorrow and pain are emphasised, even though the evil characters' plots are uncovered and Albany and Edgar insist on justice. The final devastating effects of Edmund's evil influence are felt in this scene. It is possible to argue that he is responsible for the deaths of the whole royal family, as well as his father's fate. His own death is, as Edgar seems to suggest, richly deserved. The same can be said of Gonerill and Regan's deaths.

It is hard to feel that justice is served when Cordelia's corpse is carried on, however. The good characters may have drawn together and asserted themselves, but they are unable to restore order in the way that they wish. Albany's offer to resign power might be seen as an ill-timed and futile gesture, a distraction from Lear's grief. In spite of his valour, Edgar has been unable to preserve his father's life. The final doleful lines of the play do not provide a sense of hope for the future. We are left exhausted and numb, like the characters.

As usual, Kent's tone is appropriate to the occasion. His sorrowful stoicism strikes the right note. Kent has no desire to live after his master has lost the battle, and when Lear appears himself, we know that optimism of any kind is out of place. The agony of Lear's first words, 'Howl, howl, howl! O, you are men of stones!' (line 255) expresses the misery of all the characters on stage. The repetition in Lear's lines reveals the extent of his grief and suggests that Cordelia's death is an unendurable blow. We must agree with Kent's

QUESTION

What is the dramatic justification for the deaths of Lear and Cordelia?

assessment that Lear will find release in death. Like Gloucester, he dies feeling both joy and pain. We may feel that the outcome of *King Lear* is not entirely just, but it is in many ways appropriate. All those who have sinned have certainly been punished.

GLOSSARY

13	gilded butterflies Lear is referring to superficial courtiers
84	attaint accused by
84	banns wedding banns, read publicly in church to announce a forthcoming marriage
120	canker-bit worm eaten
122	cope face, fight
129	Maugre despite
274	falchion sword

EXTENDED COMMENTARIES

TEXT 1 – II.4.212–81

GONERILL: At your choice, sir.
LEAR: I prithee, daughter, do not make me mad.
I will not trouble thee, my child. Farewell.
We'll no more meet, no more see one another.
But yet thou art my flesh, my blood, my daughter –
Or rather a disease that's in my flesh,
Which I must needs call mine. Thou art a boil,
A plague-sore, or embossed carbuncle,
In my corrupted blood. But I'll not chide thee.   220
Let shame come when it will, I do not call it.
I do not bid the thunder-bearer shoot,
Nor tell tales of thee to high-judging Jove.
Mend when thou canst, be better at thy leisure;
I can be patient, I can stay with Regan,
I and my hundred knights.
REGAN: Not altogether so.
I looked not for you yet, nor am provided

 CHECK THE BOOK
Edward Bond reworked the play as *Lear* (1971) – a bleak story set amid the building of a huge symbolic wall around a kingdom. Bond suggested that 'at death [Lear] begins to make a new life'.

For your fit welcome. Give ear, sir, to my sister;
For those that mingle reason with your passion
Must be content to think you old, and so –   230
But she knows what she does.
LEAR: Is this well spoken?
REGAN: I dare avouch it, sir. What, fifty followers?
Is it not well? What should you need of more?
Yea, or so many, sith that both charge and danger
Speak 'gainst so great a number? How in one house
Should many people under two commands
Hold amity? 'Tis hard, almost impossible.
GONERILL: Why might not you, my lord, receive attendance
From those that she calls servants, or from mine?
REGAN: Why not, my lord? If then they chanced to slack ye,   240
We could control them. If you will come to me,
For now I spy a danger, I entreat you
To bring but five-and-twenty; to no more
Will I give place or notice.
LEAR: I gave you all –
REGAN: And in good time you gave it.
LEAR: Made you my guardians, my depositaries;
But kept a reservation to be followed
With such a number. What, must I come to you
With five-and-twenty – Regan, said you so?
REGAN: And speak't again, my lord, No more with me.   250
LEAR: Those wicked creatures yet do look well-favoured
When others are more wicked. Not being the worst
Stands in some rank of praise. [*To* Gonerill] I'll go with thee.
Thy fifty yet doth double five-and-twenty,
And thou art twice her love.
GONERILL: Hear me, my lord;
What need you five-and-twenty, ten, or five
To follow, in a house where twice so many
Have a command to tend you?
REGAN: What need one?
LEAR: O, reason not the need! Our basest beggars
Are in the poorest thing superfluous.   260
Allow not nature more than nature needs –
Man's life is cheap as beast's. Thou art a lady;

CONTEXT

There had been a
period of
upheaval in
England in the
early seventeenth
century. Elizabeth I
had been
succeeded by the
son of her bitter
enemy, Mary
Queen of Scots, in
1603. The accession
of James I brought
to an end a long
period of female
rule.

> If only to go warm were gorgeous,
> Why, nature needs not what thou gorgeous wear'st,
> Which scarcely keeps thee warm. But for true need –
> You heavens, give me that patience, patience I need!
> You see me here, you gods, a poor old man,
> As full of grief as age, wretched in both;
> If it be you that stirs these daughters' hearts
> Against their father, fool me not so much   270
> To bear it tamely; touch me with noble anger,
> And let not women's weapons, water drops,
> Stain my man's cheeks. No, you unnatural hags,
> I will have such revenges on you both
> That all the world shall – I will do such things –
> What they are yet I know not; but they shall be
> The terrors of the earth. You think I'll weep.
> No, I'll not weep.
> I have full cause of weeping;
> [*storm and tempest*]
>   but this heart
> Shall break into a hundred thousand flaws   280
> Or ere I'll weep. O Fool, I shall go mad!

> **CONTEXT**
>
> Gonerill and Regan's animalism is proof of their evil natures.

This extract is a turning point for Lear. After the confrontation with Gonerill and Regan in II.4, he is driven out into the storm and goes mad. Prior to the discussion about his knights, this scene has already proved difficult for the old king. He has been treated insolently by Regan and Cornwall and his authority has been challenged. Not only has Kent been found in the stocks, but Lear's questions about his servant's punishment have also been disregarded. By the time Gonerill arrives, Lear has become an increasingly impotent figure.

We know that Lear can expect further trouble when Regan takes Gonerill's hand, greeting her warmly. The sisters are united and ready to strike. The subject of Lear's followers proves to be his undoing, as we suspected it might be when Gonerill complained about them in Act I Scene 4. Regan introduces the topic here, telling Lear repeatedly to return to Gonerill and reduce his train. To the beleaguered king his followers represent himself: his status, dignity, authority. In other words, they represent Lear as he was. By reducing their number, Gonerill and Regan show their father that he no longer has a role to play: he is nothing.

Gonerill and Regan's reduction of Lear's followers is a masterpiece of orchestrated cruelty. The sisters use a variety of hypocritical excuses to dismiss Lear's men. Regan tells Lear that 'both charge and danger / Speak 'gainst so great a number'. It would be impossible for 'two commands' in one household to 'Hold amity.' She adds that if Lear had fewer followers, they would be easier to command (but note who is to do the commanding – the new royal 'we' – Gonerill and Regan). Finally Gonerill suggests that Lear needs no one to attend him since she already has plenty of servants with 'a command to tend you'. Here we see Gonerill and Regan at their most brutally efficient. Not a word is wasted. Their (rhetorical) questions are direct and purposeful and their statements firm:

CHECK THE BOOK

For a discussion of Lear's relationship with Gonerill and Regan, see John Russell Brown, *Shakespeare: The Tragedies*, 2001.

> LEAR: Regan, said you so?
> REGAN: And speak't again, my lord. No more with me.

Impatient to get their work done, the sisters cut Lear off when he is speaking. At the end of their swift 'discussion' Regan finishes her elder sister's train of thought with a stark, short question. Their tone has been hectoring and authoritarian throughout. This is exactly what we would have expected from the sisters, having witnessed their resentful conversation at the end of Act I Scene 1. Regan is particularly vicious. Her 'And in good time you gave it' is as mean-spirited and chilling as her brazen question, 'What need one?' Regan's role as 'leader' in this scene ensures that Lear's annihilation is merciless. During Act I Scene 4 we realised Gonerill was ferocious. Now the other daughter proves herself to be every bit as callous. But what an impressive instrument of torture these two make; there is a horrible fascination in watching them at work in this scene.

At first, Lear cannot quite believe what is happening. He struggles to maintain his dignity. His opening lines to Gonerill show his desperation: 'I prithee, daughter, do not make me mad / I will not trouble thee my child. Farewell'. His politeness is pitiful. Two lines later Lear is angry again. He calls Gonerill 'a disease that's in my flesh, … a boil / A plague-sore, or embossed carbuncle'. The **imagery** of disease is apt. It accompanies the images of predatory animals used to describe Gonerill and Regan and emphasises how Lear is being assaulted by his own flesh and blood. These images are followed by thoughts of vengeance, although Lear again tries to be patient:

> … But I'll not chide thee.
> Let shame come when it will, I do not call it.
> I do not bid the thunder-bearer shoot,
> Nor tell tales of thee to high-judging Jove.

Lear hopes – understandably – that the gods will punish his ungrateful daughter. However, his insistence that he will 'tell tales' seems childish. And his tolerance is revealed as blindness when he says 'I can be patient, I can stay with Regan, / I and my hundred knights'. How little Lear has learned. He cannot shake off the idea that love is a commodity that can be bought, pleading feebly, 'I gave you all'. Lear blindly links love with money when he reminds Gonerill and Regan that he made them his 'guardians' as well as his 'depositories'. Like Edgar in the previous scene, Lear is reduced to a state of beggary, reliant on a hostile world for charity. He seems to realise this at line 259. Lear begins to speak like the helpless dependant he is:

> You heavens, give me that patience, patience I need!
> You see me here, you gods, a poor old man,
> As full of grief as age, wretched in both;
> If it be you that stirs these daughters' hearts
> Against their father, fool me not so much
> To bear it tamely

'A poor old man', Lear now has to beg for assistance. He is overwhelmed by wretchedness, terrified that his 'daughters' hearts' will defeat him. In this speech Lear also starts to consider what a man is, what true necessity means, ideas that will preoccupy him in Act III.

> **CONTEXT**
>
> James I's strong convictions about the divine right of kings are reflected in the words of a speech he made to Parliament in 1610; 'Kings are not only God's lieutenants upon earth and sit upon God's throne, but even by God himself they are called gods.'

CONTEXT

Women were at the financial mercy of men in patriarchal Renaissance Europe. They did not have independent property rights. Girls were reliant on their fathers for dowries, and once they were married, their fortunes belonged to their husbands.

But how much truth does Lear really face? His description of himself may be accurate, but he is full of self-pity, and still egotistical. He moves so quickly from considering what man needs to his own 'true need'. He sees only the sins of others. Some see Lear's request to be touched by 'noble anger' and his furious refusal to weep as signs that he is still blindly clinging to his regal persona. However, it is impossible not to pity Lear here. His struggle not to bear cruel treatment 'tamely' is impressive. Stoicism may not restore his power, but Lear's pride and fortitude can be seen as the qualities of a true tragic hero.

Lear's last speech shows the mixture of courage and fear Lear has displayed throughout Act II Scene 4. His incomplete threats, 'That all the world shall – I will do such things' are signs that Lear no longer has any control over his daughters, or his mind. But his desire for vengeance will strike a chord with the audience: Gonerill and Regan deserve to be punished. Our sympathy increases with Lear's dramatic and agonised exit, 'O Fool! I shall go mad'. The stage directions (*storm and tempest*) also provide an ominous warning of the suffering to come.

In this extract there has been an unrelenting march towards a vicious new world, where only the fittest will survive. Our fears about Gonerill and Regan have been confirmed. Regardless of the reservations we may feel about Lear and his actions, we will not be able to avoid appreciating the **pathos** of the king's situation. He has been forced to confront the truth about his daughters in a very cruel way. This extract is significant because it shows Gonerill and Regan ruthlessly in control, their energy undiminished. What new atrocities can we expect from them in Act III? There has been no sign of anything or anyone halting the progress of the evil characters, who have gained ground dramatically in Act II. This scene marks the triumph of duplicity and barbarism. As the storm starts our alarm grows.

 QUESTION

How does Shakespeare explore the theme of unkindness in the play?

TEXT 2 – III.2.1-73

LEAR: Blow, winds, and crack your cheeks! Rage! Blow!
You cataracts and hurricanoes, spout
Till you have drenched our steeples, drowned the cocks!
You sulphurous and thought-executing fires,
Vaunt-curriers of oak-cleaving thunderbolts,
Singe my white head! And thou all-shaking thunder,
Strike flat the thick rotundity o'the world,
Crack Nature's moulds, all germens spill at once
That makes ingrateful man!
FOOL: O, nuncle, court holy-water in a dry house is better than   10
this rain-water out o'door. Good nuncle, in; ask thy daughters'
blessing. Here's a night pities neither wise men nor fools.
LEAR: Rumble thy bellyful! Spit, fire! Spout, rain!
Nor rain, wind, thunder, fire are my daughters.
I tax not you, you elements, with unkindness;
I never gave you kingdom, called you children.
You owe me no subscription; then let fall
Your horrible pleasure. Here I stand, your slave,
A poor, infirm, weak and despised old man.   20
But yet I call you servile ministers,
that will with two pernicious daughters join
Your high-engendered battles 'gainst a head
So old and white as this. O, ho! 'Tis foul!
FOOL: He that has a house to put's head in has a good head-piece:

> The cod-piece that will house
> > Before the head has any,
> The head and he shall louse;
> > So beggars marry many.   30
> The man that makes his toe
> > What he his heart should make,
> Shall of a corn cry woe,
> > And turn his sleep to wake.

For there was never yet fair woman but she made mouths in
glass.

[*Enter* KENT]
LEAR: No, I will be the pattern of all patience.
I will say nothing.

CHECK THE FILM

Olivier's TV film of 1980 casts the Fool as a vulnerable and zany figure, wearing eccentric tattered clothes and spiky hair; in the BBC version of 1982 the Fool wears white face make-up like a clown and is characterised as an old retainer figure.

KENT: Who's there?

FOOL: Marry, here's grace and a cod-piece – that's a wise   40
man and a fool.

KENT: Alas, sir, are you here? Things that love night
Love not such nights as these. The wrathful skies
Gallow the very wanderers of the dark
And make them keep their caves. Since I was man,
Such sheets of fire, such bursts of horrid thunder,
Such groans of roaring wind and rain I never
Remember to have heard. Man's nature cannot carry
Th'affliction not the fear.

LEAR: Let the great gods
That keep this dreadful pudder o'er our heads   50
Find out their enemies now. Tremble, thou wretch
That hast within thee undivulgèd crimes
Unwhipped of justice. Hide thee, thou bloody hand,
Thou perjured, and thou simular of virtue
That art incestuous. Caitiff, to pieces shake,
That under covert and convenient seeming
Has practised on man's life. Close pent-up guilts,
Rive your concealing continents, and cry
These dreadful summoners grace. I am a man
More sinned against than sinning.   60

KENT: Alack, bare-headed?
Gracious my lord, hard by here is a hovel;
Some friendship will it lend you 'gainst the tempest.
Repose you there while I to this hard house –
More harder than the stones whereof 'tis raised;
Which even but now, demanding after you,
Denied me to come in – return and force
Their scanted courtesy.

LEAR: My wits begin to turn.
Come on, my boy. How dost my boy? Art cold?
I am cold myself. Where is the straw, my fellow?
The art of our necessities is strange   70
And can make vile things precious. Come, your hovel.
Poor fool and knave, I have one part in my heart
That's sorry yet for thee.

CHECK THE FILM

In Grigori Kozintsev's Russian version (1970) the Fool survives the events but is poignantly mute for the second half of the play, turning into a village idiot figure mourning the loss of his world.

In this scene the style and structure of Lear's speeches convey the king's confused and violent state of mind. We see anger, a desire for revenge, egotism, and more positively, humility and a recognition of previous mistakes. Lear's speeches also reflect the movements of the storm. Lear's opening line, 'Blow, winds … Rage, blow' is like a crack of thunder, suggesting that Shakespeare is using Lear's language to create the effects of the storm for the audience. Lear *is* the storm. His actions have led to misrule in the kingdom, and nature reflects that chaos. Lear has made others suffer, now the storm makes him suffer.

Lear wants to see the world destroyed by 'cataracts and hurricanoes' because of the treachery of 'ingrateful man'. These last two words indicate that Lear blames Gonerill and Regan for his suffering. But he also seems to welcome his own destruction when he yells, 'Singe my white head!'. Perhaps this is an acknowledgement of his sins, a desire to be punished for his folly. However, Lear continues to act out the role of mighty monarch. His first speech is a long list of commands. He expects the tempest to do his bidding. Has Lear really woken up to his errors? Lear's second speech is less explosive, but still full of rage:

> I tax not you, you elements, with unkindness;
> I never gave you kingdom, called you children.
> You owe me no subscription; then let fall
> Your horrible pleasure.

Now Lear recognises that he cannot rule the elements. He says – with crazy egotism – that they owe him 'no subscription'. These lines continue the theme of 'ingrateful man' and sum up the lunatic king's version of events so far. Lear's words convey the self-pity he feels: 'Here I stand, your slave, / A poor, infirm, weak, and despised old man'. This description might be seen as the accurate self-assessment of a man who is beginning to see himself more clearly. All the adjectives are bleak, with a particularly stark final choice: despised. Lear's reference to himself as a 'slave' is significant too. In Act II Scene 4 he said he would rather work as Oswald's slave than return to Gonerill. Now he begins to see that he has – indeed is –

 CHECK THE NET
A good site which has a lot on the Renaissance context, and many links to other relevant material, including Bradley (see **Critical approaches**) is **www.stjohns-chs.org/library/ curriculum/ English/renaiss/ ren.html**.

CONTEXT

The full title of the play as published in 1608 – *The History of King Lear and his Three Daughters* – makes it sound like a fairy tale, and there are elements of folk stories in the play including echoes of Cinderella and the Ugly Sisters. These parallels may encourage us to think that, like Cinderella, all will be well for Cordelia in the end, too.

nothing. His paranoid delusion that the storm is in league with his 'pernicious daughters' seems to confirm his arrogant vulnerability.

The violence of the storm and his daughters' treachery push Lear into considering other violent or unnatural criminals who remain 'Unwhipped of justice'. He starts to look at the lives of those he was responsible for as ruler through new eyes, struggling to understand the world that has been revealed to him. However, Lear returns to himself again in the final lines of this speech: 'I am a man / More sinned against than sinning'. This statement needs careful consideration. Is it true? Given the events of the final moments of the play, the judgement is likely to go in Lear's favour.

While Lear welcomes the storm, Kent and the Fool show us how dreadful its effects are and guide our responses to Lear. Kent is aghast when he finds his master 'bare-headed'. The fact that Lear runs about 'unbonneted' indicates how weak he is, and shows how far he has fallen since the start of Act I, when he had his crown and all the other trappings of majesty to protect him. Now Lear is mentally and physically exposed. When Lear tries to remove his clothing in Act III Scene 4 he deliberately chooses to humble himself further and moves closer to empathising with the plight of 'unaccommodated man'. Kent's speech at lines 42–9 serves two purposes. His descriptions of the storm, with its 'sheets of fire', 'horrid thunder' and 'groans of roaring wind and rain' bring the tempest more vividly to life for the audience and reinforce its dangers. We are told that 'Man's nature cannot carry / Th'affliction nor the fear of nights like these'. The Fool, who finds the storm very hard to bear, urges Lear to return and 'ask thy daughters' blessing'. For the Fool to ask Lear to submit to his daughters, things must indeed be desperate on the heath. This desperation is forced home when Kent seems to suggest the same course of action at line 63. The Fool's vulnerability also heightens and reflects Lear's. He shows us an attractive side of Lear's character. The king now finds time to feel for another, 'Come on, my boy. How dost my boy? Art cold? ... Poor fool and knave, I have one part in my heart / That's sorry yet for thee'. These lines will impress the audience, although Lear is still obviously caught up in his own sufferings (only 'one part' of his heart feels sorry for the Fool). But who can blame Lear for focusing on his own agony here? It is clear that he is increasingly isolated in his madness. He hardly acknowledges his companions on the heath until he speaks to the Fool at line 68.

This scene is significant for several reasons. It shows us Lear in the first stages of his madness and we see the outcome we expected at the end of Act II Scene 4. We learn that Lear is preoccupied by thoughts about filial ingratitude but also considers broader questions as he struggles to retain his wits. We see him start to move towards greater self-awareness in spite of his continued egotism. Lear becomes more generous. The storm reflects the terrible state England is now in, ruled by cruel monsters. The hostile setting and violent **imagery** increase our fears about events to come and make us fear for Lear's safety. How will the king survive this night, which seems so unendurable? This scene also offers us a faint glimmer of hope about human nature. The Fool and Kent stick by their master, the Fool calling Lear by the affectionate name 'nuncle' and Kent insisting on addressing Lear respectfully as 'my lord'. These flashes of compassion are vital in Act III, which closes with an act of appalling inhumanity.

QUESTION

By what means does Shakespeare arouse our feelings of pity in this play?

TEXT 3 – IV.7.30–84

CORDELIA: Had you not been their father, these white flakes   30
Did challenge pity of them. Was this a face
To be opposed against the jarring winds?
To stand against the deep dread-bolted thunder,
In the most terrible and nimble stroke
Of quick cross lightning? To watch, poor perdu,
With this thin helm? Mine enemy's dog,
Though he had bit me, should have stood that night
Against my fire; and wast thou fain, poor father,
To hovel thee with swine and rogues forlorn
In short and musty straw? Alack, alack!   40
'Tis wonder that thy life and wits at once
Had not concluded all. – He wakes! Speak to him.
DOCTOR: Madam, do you; 'tis fittest.
CORDELIA: How does my royal lord? How fares your majesty?
LEAR: You do me wrong to take me out o'the grave.

Thou art a soul in bliss; but I am bound
Upon a wheel of fire, that mine own tears
Do scald like molten lead.
CORDELIA: Sir, do you know me?
LEAR: You are a spirit, I know. Where did you die?
CORDELIA: Still, still far wide!   50
DOCTOR: He's scarce awake. Let him alone awhile.
LEAR: Where have I been? Where am I? Fair daylight?
I am mightily abused. I should even die with pity
To see another thus. I know not what to say.
I will not swear these are my hands. Let's see.
I feel this pin-prick. Would I were assured
Of my condition.
CORDELIA: O look upon me, sir,
And hold your hand in benediction o'er me.
[LEAR *falls to his knees*]
No, sir, you must not kneel.
LEAR: Pray do not mock me.
I am a very foolish fond old man,   60
Four score and upward, not an hour more nor less,
And, to deal plainly,
I fear I am not in my perfect mind.
Methinks I should know you, and know this man;
Yet I am doubtful; for I am mainly ignorant
What this place is; and all the skill I have
Remembers not these garments; nor I know not
Where I did lodge last night. Do not laugh at me,
For, as I am a man, I think this lady
To be my child Cordelia.
CORDELIA: [*weeping*]   And so I am, I am.   70
LEAR: Be your tears wet? Yes, faith! I pray, weep not.
If you have poison for me I will drink it.
I know you do not love me, for your sisters
Have, as I do remember, done me wrong.
You have some cause; they have not.
CORDELIA: No cause, no cause.
LEAR: Am I in France?
KENT: In your own kingdom, sir.
LEAR: Do not abuse me.

CHECK THE FILM

In Olivier's 1980 TV version, the reunion of Cordelia and Lear is uplit from the snowy-white sheets under which Lear lies sleeping. His vulnerability is symbolised by the fact that his beard has been shaved off – perhaps allying him with the beard-plucked Gloucester in the blinding scene.

DOCTOR: Be comforted, good madam. The great rage,
You see, is killed in him; and yet it is danger
To make him even o'er the time he has lost.   80
Desire him to go in; trouble him no more
Till further settling.
CORDELIA: Will't please your highness walk?
LEAR: You must bear with me. Pray you now, forget and forgive.
I am old and foolish.

This quiet and moving scene comes as a relief after the violent struggles of Act III, and the harsh comedy of Gloucester and Lear's final meeting in Act IV Scene 6. We are prepared for a scene of reconciliation by Kent's conversation with the Gentleman in Act IV Scene 3. Here we learned that Lear was so ashamed of 'his own unkindness' that he would not see Cordelia (IV.3.42–5). Other dramatic devices also point towards restoration. Music is being played, and as Lear is carried in wearing fresh garments, all the characters on stage fall to their knees, reaffirming Lear's status as king. Cordelia kneels at her father's side and kisses his hand. This gesture of love and pity sets the tone for the scene to come.

Cordelia's speech at line 30 is her last long speech in the play. Her sole concern is Lear. As she describes Lear's sufferings in the storm we are reminded of Gonerill and Regan's cruelty. When Cordelia asks 'Was this a face / To be opposed against the jarring winds?' we will share her outrage. Finally, we are reminded how far the 'poor perdu' has fallen when Cordelia laments the way her father had to 'hovel thee … / In short and musty straw' (lines 39–40). These sorrowful descriptions highlight Lear's vulnerability and reaffirm Cordelia's virtuous nature. Her warmth and compassion contrast sharply with her sisters' cold vindictiveness. Cordelia's modesty is shown when she asks the Doctor to speak to Lear first. She seems as reluctant to speak now as she was in Act I Scene 1. Are we to assume that Cordelia still finds it hard to express her love? Perhaps she shrinks from speaking because she is nervous about how her 'child-changed' father will react when he sees her. Cordelia's request to the Doctor provides a last moment of tension before the reconciliation.

 CHECK THE NET

This site is a comprehensive Penguin study guide to the play. It is aimed primarily at teachers, but there is a lot of material that would be useful to A-level students and undergraduates too. There is information on Shakespeare's language in *Lear*, and some study questions to help students think about the play as they are reading it. There are lists of quotations linked to the themes of the play, and some comments on themes that compliment the **Themes** section. **http:// cn. penguinclassics. com/shared/ SharedDisplay/ 0,,49840_0,00.htm**

QUESTION

Are there any
heroes in *King
Lear*?

When Lear wakes up Cordelia's anxious questions, 'How does my
royal lord? How fares your majesty?' indicate that she now submits
to her father's authority. The formal distance of these words is
softened by the possessive 'my', which suggests Cordelia's desire to
re-establish a close relationship with Lear. She urgently wants to be
recognised and is upset when she realises her father is 'Still, still far
wide' (line 50). She continues to seem choked for the rest of the
scene; falling to her knees and begging for Lear's blessing, and then
weeping during Lear's hesitant self-appraisal at line 60. After this
she is so overwrought that she can only offer a brief 'No cause, no
cause' (line 75) and ask gently if her father will take a walk with her
(but only if it pleases him). In Act IV Scene 7 Cordelia seems to be
the perfect, doting daughter. Her submissiveness suggests to some
modern critics that Shakespeare has started to rehabilitate and
reaffirm the patriarchal hierarchy in the final scenes of the play.
Cordelia's insistence that she has no reason to hate Lear confirms,
perhaps, that the authority he exercised over in Act I Scene 1 has
now been accepted as just. Alternatively, we might see her gentle
pity as redemptive, and her 'No cause, no cause' as the natural
response of a caring daughter.

Lear's lines indicate that the king is now a figure of **pathos**. His first
speech shows his relentless suffering:

> You do me wrong to take me out o' the grave.
> Thou are a soul in bliss; but I am bound
> Upon a wheel of fire, that mine own tears
> Do scald like molten lead.

Life is torturous for Lear. He has finally given in to weeping and is
utterly bewildered by what he sees. He says that he cannot piece
together the events of the previous twenty four hours and murmurs
helplessly, 'I know not what to say'. Perhaps Lear has learned the
lesson that Cordelia was trying to teach him in I.1, that language
cannot express emotions truly. He is humbled. This humility is
continued in other lines. Although Lear continues to speak largely
about himself in a self-pitying tone, he looks outwards too. He says
that he would hate 'To see another thus' and expresses doubts about
his senses. He sums himself up with devastating simplicity; he is 'a

very foolish, fond old man ... not in my perfect mind'. Most significantly, he attempts to kneel before Cordelia and recognises that she has 'some cause' for hating him. It might also be argued that Lear's use of first person pronouns, 'methinks' and 'I', suggests greater humility. Gone is the earlier use of the omnipotent third person, the royal 'we'. Lear seems to have accepted his diminished status. When he offers to drink poison even the most hard-hearted spectator will be moved to tears. Lear's self-pity seems acceptable now – he has suffered so deeply.

Lear's view of himself is altogether more realistic than the version of Lear Cordelia responds to. The simplicity of the king's language reflects his diminished status. Lear shuns anything that smacks of regality, denying that he has any authority:

> LEAR: Am I in France?
> KENT: In your own kingdom, sir.
> LEAR: Do not abuse me.

It is too late. Fresh garments cannot restore Lear to his former glory. Lear is now more concerned with 'my child Cordelia'. We are being prepared for Act V Scene 3, when Lear acts out the role of protective father.

We are pulled in two ways in this scene. Cordelia and Lear express the same emotions: pain, humility, concern. Their mutual caring is shown by the way they finish off each other's lines (Cordelia constantly tries to reassure her father, as at line 75). When they leave the stage together it seems that the reconciliation is complete. Lear has finally achieved his heart's desire; he can now rely on Cordelia's 'kind nursery'. This outcome provides us with a sense of relief. But we also doubt that Lear will survive long. He no longer speaks or acts like a mighty king. Every line he delivers confirms his weakness. Cordelia's reverence is ultimately rather hopeless.

This scene is significant because we see a fragile family harmony restored when Cordelia is reclaimed. Lear no longer holds false values. He recognises love and goodness accurately. We welcome his increased wisdom and humility. Act IV Scene 7 also provides an

---

CONTEXT

Many would argue that *King Lear* is an unusual tragedy because instead of seeing a good but flawed man fall (as in *Othello*), we watch as a tyrant moves towards a conciliatory ending, where he is reunited with the person he loves most.

CONTEXT

Many of Shakespeare's sources for the play give it a happy ending – including the earlier play *The True Chronicle History of King Lear and his Daughters* – in which Lear and Cordelia are reunited and the king restored to the throne. Maybe Shakespeare is drawing deliberately on these optimistic expectations just in order to dash our hopes in the final bleak conclusion.

outlet for the pity we have felt for the old king since the end of Act II. Cordelia's tears guide our responses and foreshadow Lear's agonised mourning of Act V Scene 3. Finally, this scene points towards the restoration of the hierarchy that occurs at the end of *King Lear*. As the play moves into Act V we wait anxiously to see whether Cordelia's virtues or Gonerill and Regan's vices will triumph.

PART THREE

CRITICAL APPROACHES

CHARACTERISATION

Although characters are presented as individuals it is important to remember that some are based on familiar dramatic types from Renaissance drama. Edmund is partly **malcontent, Machiavellian** villain, the Fool is 'all-licensed' jester, whose role it is to comment on the action. Because of the functions they serve in the plot, characters sometimes appear to act inconsistently. For example, Edmund decides to do good at the end of the play. Why? He says he is moved by Edgar's description of Gloucester's death. But we must not forget that Shakespeare needs Edmund to act virtuously in order to increase dramatic tension – will Cordelia and Lear be spared?

Shakespeare is not primarily concerned with motives; he is more interested in the effects of characters' decisions and natures. In *King Lear* he focuses on the tragic consequences of two fathers' actions, and how events shape their characters. During the course of the play the other characters also change and grow; some are good and become better, others are bad and become more depraved. Lear and Gloucester are exceptions. Neither is good or bad in a straightforward way. Lear's **characterisation** is particularly complex. He is not a tragic hero with a single tragic flaw which causes his downfall. Nor is his growth a simple movement from ignorance to knowledge. When he emerges from his madness Lear may have learned a great deal, but doubts remain about the depth of his understanding. Our responses to Lear are complex too. He is infuriating in Act I Scene 1, becoming increasingly sympathetic as he suffers.

It is also worth remembering that interpretations of character cannot be set in stone. Each age sees the characters through its own eyes, and each time *King Lear* is performed on stage, directors and actors bring their own ideas to the text. Thus it is possible to have a range of Lears, Cordelias, Edmunds. As a reader you need to focus

CHECK THE FILM

The film based on the novel by Jane Smiley, *A Thousand Acres* (1997) updates the *Lear* story to a large farm in Iowa. Told by the sympathetic Gonerill equivalent, Ginny, the film tells the story from a viewpoint the play does not allow us, offering a unique perspective on the characters of Lear and Cordelia.

on what characters say, the language they use, and how they interact.

LEAR

CONTEXT

In the Quarto version of the play, Lear speaks of dividing his land into three separate 'kingdomes'. In the Folio, Lear intends splitting his 'kingdome' in three. Scholars have suggested that the wording in the Quarto would have been particularly alarming to the Jacobean audience, who had been nervous about England's fate when Elizabeth I died. In particular, they had been concerned about the possibility of civil war.

As suggested above, Lear is a complex tragic hero, who excites a variety of responses. Watching his disastrous actions of Act I Scene 1 it is hard not to feel that Lear deserves punishment for his folly. He displays many traits designed to alienate an audience. Quick to vituperative anger when displeased and too arrogant to take advice, Lear is blind and irresponsible as father and ruler. His 'darker purpose' would have alarmed the Jacobean audience, who would remember how the taxing question of the succession had loomed large during the reign of Elizabeth I. Lear attempts to divide power from responsibility. He is preoccupied with appearances. If he can retain the trappings of majesty without the 'cares and business' of ruling he is content. We realise early how false his values are. It is also possible to see his desire to rely on Cordelia's 'kind nursery' (I.1.124) as selfish. He intends marrying her off in Act I Scene 1 but expects to be nursed while he crawls 'unburdened' (I.1.41) towards death. Lear is both tyrannical patriarch and demanding child at the start of the play.

And yet we sympathise with this egotistical autocrat. In Act II Lear's better qualities are revealed. His hiring of Kent/Caius is a sign that Lear inspires loyalty, and his interaction with the Fool shows a more tolerant side to his nature. It also becomes clear that Lear is trying to remain calm even when he feels he is being wronged (I.4.56–70). In the next scene Lear recognises that he has behaved foolishly and treated Cordelia unkindly (I.5.24). As his insight and troubles grow, so does our concern. We begin to share his outrage as Gonerill and Regan become more repugnant. There is desperation as well as egotism in his confrontation with his 'dog-hearted' (IV.3.00) daughters in Act II Scene 4. Gradually Lear's rages become signs of impotence, not authority. By the time he rushes out into the storm our sympathies are likely to lie – and remain – with the beleaguered king.

Many critics see Lear's insanity as a learning process. Lear needs to suffer to improve his understanding of himself and the society in which he lives. Certainly he considers a number of topics he paid little attention to: the wretched condition of the poor, the corrupt justice system, true necessity. He learns to distinguish between appearances and reality and considers the sufferings of those close to him. Lear also becomes much more self-critical. He emerges from his torment a more humble, loving and attractive character.

However, other commentators suggest that Lear remains self-obsessed and vengeful. His philosophical enquiries on the heath are punctuated by thoughts of punishing Gonerill and Regan. Again and again he returns to the crimes committed against him. He struggles to accept responsibility for his elder daughters' cruel natures and never fully acknowledges the folly of his actions of I.1.

We are not allowed to remain too critical though. His reconciliation with Cordelia shows the best of Lear. Ashamed of his former unkindness, he humbles himself before his youngest daughter, acknowledging her superiority. We can forgive him now focusing on the way he has been abused. At the end of the play Lear seems to move beyond himself. He has certainly accepted his powerless, diminished status and now sees himself primarily as Cordelia's father. His language reflects his progress. Gone is the royal 'we'. Now Lear uses the first person when he speaks of himself and his feelings. Cordelia is reclaimed lovingly as 'my Cordelia' (V.3.20). In Act V Lear clings to his 'best object' (I.1.214) protectively. He revenges her death by killing the 'slave' responsible for hanging her. In all of his speeches in V.3 the dying king focuses on Cordelia and the overwhelming grief he feels at her passing. Lear's love for and defence of Cordelia go a long way to redeeming him from charges of egotism. Lear has clearly learned the value of true emotion. His recognition of the injustice of Cordelia's death suggests that his judgement has been restored (V.3.304–5). But wisdom comes too late. Watching the final bleak moments of the play it is easy to feel that Lear's sufferings have been in vain.

GONERILL AND REGAN

Lear's elder daughters are very subversive figures. Initially, Gonerill seems to be the dominant sister. She decides that something must be done to ensure that Lear's rough treatment of Cordelia does not

CONTEXT

The traditional structure of a classical tragedy (upon which Shakespeare and his contemporaries based their tragedies), highlights the isolation of the protagonist. Is this what happens to King Lear as he loses his wits?

CHECK THE BOOK

For a 'purgatorial' reading of the play, which compares Lear to the biblical figure Job, see G. Wilson Knight's *The Wheel of Fire*, Routledge, 1989.

extend to Regan and herself. It is also Gonerill who raises the issue of Lear's knights and provokes the first confrontation with her father in Act I Scene 4. Up to this point Regan seems happy to follow Gonerill's course of action. But we get hints of her particular brand of sadism in Act I Scene 2 when she urges Cornwall to inflict further punishment on Kent. And then in Act II Scene 4 she leads the onslaught against Lear. The sisters are now vicious equals. Both participate in what is for many the most horrific scene in the play, the blinding of Gloucester. Gonerill suggests the method of torture, 'Pluck out his ... eyes!' (III.7.56), and then Regan assaults Gloucester, egging her husband on to further cruelty.

Gonerill and Regan share many character traits. Both are threatening and autocratic, cold and ambitious. Both lust after Edmund in a predatory and unfeminine way. They are masculine in other ways. Gonerill denies Albany's authority and arrogantly asserts her own power when she says, 'the laws are mine, not thine' (V.3.156). Regan may not be an adulteress, but she is a murderess, like her sister. She does man's work when she runs the servant through in Act III Scene 7. Gonerill and Regan's vindictive assertiveness would have been particularly shocking to a Jacobean audience. Renaissance models of femininity required women to be quiet and submissive. Lear's daughters subvert all the accepted codes of feminine behaviour. They set out to destroy the family and the state. They are agents of chaos and misrule. The terror the sisters inspire is emphasised by the animal **imagery** in the play and by the abhorrence of female sexuality exhibited, especially by Lear. Ultimately we are supposed to reject Gonerill and Regan utterly. We might recognise the validity of their complaints about Lear in Act I Scene 1; we might momentarily sympathise with them because they are not Lear's favourites, but we still abhor them. Even Edmund comments on their bad natures. Jealous, treacherous, immoral; these two display all the most distressing features of inhumanity, murdering and maiming without remorse. The best that can be said for Gonerill and Regan is that they are energetic in their pursuit of self-gratification. There is a horrible fascination in watching them at work.

CORDELIA

Lear's favourite daughter is possibly more problematical for audiences today than she would have been for the Jacobean theatregoer. She can seem infuriatingly pious. Why does she refuse to take part in Lear's love-test, when she knows how evil Gonerill and Regan are? Can we blame her for the violence and cruelty of her sisters' reign? And what of Cordelia's subversion of Lear's authority? These are awkward questions. Some critics interpret her refusal to speak flattering words to Lear and her acceptance of France as acts of defiance; she is in direct conflict with patriarchy on both occasions, refusing to submit to her father's will. Her stubborn 'Nothing' (I.1.87) leads the way for Gonerill and Regan's rebellion. If we follow these arguments through it is possible to interpret Cordelia's death as a reward for her early disobedience. These, however, are extreme views, which do not really fit in with the portrayal of Cordelia's character in Acts IV and V, or with the consistently high esteem in which Cordelia is held by the good characters. Remember, France takes her for her virtues alone.

It is also necessary to look at Cordelia's motives in Act I Scene 1. She is seeking to alert Lear to his poor judgement. Her refusal to participate in a glib public-speaking contest can be seen as a sign of her integrity. As the play progresses we learn to distrust all the characters who have an easy way with words. Cordelia's 'Nothing' (I.1.87) looks increasingly honest and worthy. When she returns in Act IV Cordelia is anything but subversive. In the Quarto we are prepared for her reappearance by Kent and the Gentleman, who stress her feminine beauty and modesty and the pain she feels when hearing about Lear's sufferings. We are presented with a perfect daughter who will act as redeemer. In Act IV Scene 7 she is solicitous and respectful towards her father, restored as Lear's 'best object' (I.1.214). It is probably this Cordelia we remember; the selfless daughter, full of pity and love. When Lear carries on her corpse, yelling in agony, we are appalled. Like Lear we want to know why 'a dog, a horse, a rat have life / And thou no breath at all?' (V.3.304–5).

Cordelia's death has troubled critics and audiences since the play was first performed. There are various ways of explaining it.

> **CONTEXT**
>
> Some critics have suggested that Kent and Cordelia's behaviour in Act I Scene 1 can be read as a warning to James I not to be taken in by flattering courtiers and advisors. Like his predecessor, Elizabeth I, James was to gain a reputation for indulging his favourites.

CHECK THE NET

www.ukc.ac.uk/
secl/german/
ge501lk.html
is a site which has
materials on
European tragedies.
Extensive materials
on *King Lear* – the
play as tragedy,
heroism in the play
and very good
analysis of the
characters –
especially Cordelia
and the villains. This
site will help
students consider
the play and its
characters from
different
perspectives.

Shakespeare needs a final cruel blow to bring about Lear's death. Perhaps Cordelia's death is an expression of the playwright's tragic vision. It might also be a final example of man's inhumanity to man in the world of *King Lear*. Shakespeare perhaps wants to show the full horror of the consequences of Lear's folly. For some, Cordelia's death is the real **tragedy** of *King Lear*.

Our assessment of Cordelia should probably conclude that although she is as stubborn as the rest of her family, she is a paragon in comparison with her sisters. In two telling lines Lear says 'Her voice was ever soft / Gentle and low – an excellent thing in a woman' (V.3.270–1). It is impossible to imagine Lear's other two 'dog-hearted' (IV.3.45) daughters ever being described in this way. Cordelia's **characterisation** goes some way to counteract the vicious, masculine cruelty of Gonerill and Regan, and the abhorrence of the female so prevalent in the play. We would probably agree that her death is worth avenging.

GLOUCESTER

Gloucester has some individual features – his superstition, his adultery – but his character is determined largely by the parallel role he plays. Like Lear, he is a complacent father, used to assuming authority. Like Lear, Gloucester acts rashly and ruthlessly when he believes that his son Edgar has rebelled against him, putting himself in his evil son's power. Like Lear, Gloucester fails to 'keep his house in order'. His adultery might be seen as a failure to take his patriarchal responsibilities seriously. He is as blind as his ruler.

Gloucester seems to lack resolution for much of Act II. He tries vainly to keep the peace between Lear and his daughters and it is difficult not to judge him harshly when his doors are shut against the king. All he can offer are faint-hearted protests (II.4.295–7). But Gloucester also displays more positive qualities. When he takes action he is brave and determined. He helps Lear on the heath, providing a litter to transport him to safety. Gloucester is heroic in Act III Scene 7, denouncing Gonerill and Regan ferociously. He proves that he can be stoical in the face of monstrous cruelty. When he learns the truth about Edmund his tormented desire to be reconciled with Edgar redeems him. Like Lear, Gloucester becomes increasingly generous as he suffers. He expresses great pity for Lear in Act IV and is genuinely concerned about the dangers the old man and Poor Tom face when helping him. His developing concern for social justice mirrors Lear's.

Gloucester's pain and despair reflect Lear's. While the lunatic king raves about his daughters Gloucester confesses sadly that he is 'almost mad' (III.4.159) himself, thinking about Edgar's supposed treachery. Even after his 'fall' at Dover cliff and his agreement to 'bear / Affliction till it do cry out itself / "Enough, enough", and die' (IV.6.75–7) Gloucester remains suicidal. He welcomes Oswald's sword and is still deeply depressed as late as Act V Scene 2. His dark thoughts play a key role in establishing and maintaining the bleak atmosphere of the second half of the play. Gloucester's pessimistic lines often seem prophetic: 'This great world / Shall so wear out to naught' (IV.6.135–6). His willingness to die perhaps points towards the carnage of Act V Scene 3, preparing us for the final tragic outcome. His death can be seen as a 'dry run' for Lear's. Some critics see Lear's passing as a mirror image of Gloucester's. The old earl dies when his 'flawed heart – / Alack, too weak the conflict to support – / 'Twixt two extremes of passion, joy and grief, / Burst smilingly' (V.3.194–7). The reconciliation with Edgar is too much to bear.

Gloucester is punished very harshly for his misjudgements of character. Edgar's verdict, that he dies for adultery, is not easily accepted. For all his faults, Gloucester will probably be viewed by most audiences as a character more sinned against than sinning.

EDGAR

Many critics feel dissatisfied with Edgar. He plays so many roles and performs such a wide range of functions; is he simply a plot device? Shakespeare does not spend much time establishing Edgar's virtues before having him disguise himself as Poor Tom. Gloucester's legitimate son starts the play a passive, credulous dupe upon whom Edmund's devious practices ride easy. In Act I he shows none of the heroism he displays later in the play. So how are we to view his lightning changes?

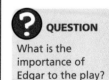

QUESTION

What is the importance of Edgar to the play?

It is possible to detect progression in Edgar's **characterisation** as he moves from one role to another. He grows in stature through his use of disguises. He is forced to assume the garb of a madman to preserve his life, but his final disguise – masked avenger – enables him to take command of his own fate. Those who complain of Edgar's weak gullibility also forget that Jacobean audiences would have understood that good characters were easy to fool. Villains were accepted as being so cunning that their evil intentions were impossible to detect. Edgar's willingness to be guided by Edmund might be seen as proof of his worthiness.

CONTEXT

Strict Puritans believed that death was the appropriate punishment for adultery. Does this make Edgar a religious extremist?

On the heath the role of lunatic beggar pushes Edgar centre stage. Many critics have noticed how the presence of the fake madman helps Lear. As he interacts with Poor Tom, Lear's humanity and understanding increase. Edgar also comments on Lear and Gloucester's suffering, guiding audience responses to the two patriarchs in Acts III and IV. He is actively generous too. In Act IV Edgar guides Gloucester and tries to chase away his gloomy thoughts. Like Cordelia, Edgar feels only sympathy for the father who rejected him so brutally. At the end of Act IV Scene 6 Edgar's role-playing enables him to defend Gloucester when Oswald threatens him. To preserve Edgar's moral character (revengers in Jacobean drama often have sinister motives) Shakespeare shows us his remorse. His valour awakened, Edgar is now ready to challenge Edmund. His facility with language has been used to protect himself and others. His deceptions are essentially honest.

In Act V Edgar becomes an agent of justice. He helps to restore the old order. It is possible to view Edgar as the only character unsullied enough to rule after Lear's death. He has committed no crime against his family or the state. He has never questioned the authority of his elders. He took action when necessary. The worst we can accuse Edgar of is leaving it very late to reveal himself to Gloucester, and he is heartily sorry for this. Edgar has endured appalling privation and shown mercy and strength. When he speaks of his journey through the play as a 'pilgrimage' (V.3.194) we understand the serious sense of purpose behind Edgar's role-playing. Surely he has proved himself many times over? When he unassumingly takes charge we have some justification for feeling that his succession is acceptable.

Some doubts remain. His uncompromising judgement of his father's 'crimes' is disturbing. What has happened to his Christian pity? His belief that the gods are just looks decidedly suspect when Cordelia dies. In comparison with the titanic Lear, Edgar can also seem lacklustre. Our reception of his character depends heavily upon how he is played on stage. In performance Edgar's heroic qualities can be stressed, and his disparate parts can be forged into a more or less satisfactory whole.

EDMUND

Like many villains in Jacobean drama, Edmund seethes with frustration about the 'plague of custom' (I.2.3) that keeps him on the fringes of society. His **Machiavellian** qualities include his political ambition and willingness to use unscrupulous methods to achieve his aims. As Edmund says himself, he is adaptable and ready to manipulate events to serve his turn; 'all with me's meet / that I can fashion fit' (I.2.180). His ability to adopt the right tone in any situation helps him in his progress towards power.

But does Edmund really set himself up against the society he operates in, as some critics suggest? Certainly he sneers at its values, as his toying with the words 'base' and 'legitimate' shows (see I.2.10 and I.2.18–19). Edmund seems to subscribe to a savage code: survival of the fittest. His goddess, Nature, is a brutal, anarchic force. Edmund never apologises for his wickedness; he revels in it right up to the final scene. All the beliefs he outlines in Act I Scene 2 suggest he rejects the hierarchy that has made his father and brother so prosperous. But his own ambitions are worldly; really, he wants to succeed in society's terms. He aims first at Edgar's inheritance, then at Gloucester's title and finally at the throne of England. Surely Edmund cannot therefore be viewed as an anti-establishment figure?

Yet Edmund is subversive. The alacrity of his rise is an indication of this. He is very successful in Gonerill and Regan's cruel world. He is responsible for the deaths of three princesses, as well as the cruel maiming of his father. His progress is halted too late to save Lear. By the end of the final scene Edmund has proved himself to be formidably destructive. He almost obtains everything he wants.

> **CONTEXT**
>
> The tale of the good and bad brother was a frequently used folk motif, which would have been very familiar to Shakespeare's audience.

**CHECK
THE FILM**

In many film and TV productions, Edmund is shot in close up, delivering his **soliloquies** directly to camera. Thus, the audience is encouraged to see how seductive and persuasive the villain can be.

However, we come to loathe everything Edmund stands for. We may admire his tenacity and quick wits, enjoy his energetic acting out of roles and the way he takes us into his confidence through his use of **soliloquies**; but we must reject him, as we reject Gonerill and Regan. In Act V Scene 3 Edmund is defeated when Albany and Edgar reassert the values of the old order. Now Edmund is forced to reject his code and submit. His fall is as meteoric as his rise. We know his subversion has failed when we hear him say he will forgive his deathsman if he is of noble blood. His dying desire to do good also seems to cancel out his earlier delight in his own villainy. Edmund's strange last line, 'Yet Edmund was beloved' (V.3.237) might be read as confirming the virtuous characters' insistence throughout the play that caring and loyalty are important. Few will regret the defiant bastard son's demise.

THE FOOL

The Fool plays a number of roles: voice of conscience, social commentator, truth-teller, representative of Cordelia, vehicle for **pathos**, Lear's alter-ego, dramatic **chorus**. His songs, riddles and epigrams also provide comic relief. The flippant remark about Poor Tom's clothing is a good example of the Fool lightening the tone of a distressing scene (III.4.60–1). Many of the Fool's other speeches can be played for comic effect, but it is possible to stress the 'bitter' rather than the witty fool. When he first appears in the play the Fool is extremely critical of Lear: 'Dost thou call me fool, boy? / All thy other titles thou hast given away; that thou wast born with' (1.4.146–8). These lines are typical of the Fool's interaction with Lear. His sarcasm is blunt and hard hitting. The Fool's bitterness can partly be understood by considering his role as Cordelia's representative. A truth-teller, like Lear's youngest daughter, he pines away when she goes to France. Many of the Fool's early cutting speeches are designed to alert Lear to his daughters' true characters. However, unlike Cordelia, the Fool is never punished for his truth telling. He is 'all-licensed' (I.4.196). Jesters were often kept by the monarch to provide witty analysis of contemporary behaviour and to remind the sovereign of his humanity. Certainly Lear's Fool fulfils these functions for his master. He also enjoys a close and affectionate relationship with 'nuncle' Lear (II.4.117). It is the Fool Lear calls out to when he fears he is going mad. On the heath the king considers his servant's sufferings alongside his own. In return the Fool remains steadfastly loyal. In a play where family relationships are disastrously bad, the Fool seems to play the role of good son.

The Fool's role as social commentator has been linked to the prophecy he makes at the end of Act III Scene 2. In this speech the Fool comments on the injustices and corruption of Lear's reign (III.2.79–96) and perhaps predicts a better time to come. Throughout the play he draws attention to the chaos Lear has caused in the kingdom by making his daughters his mothers. The implication of many of his speeches is that Lear has wronged the country as well as himself.

Some critics wonder whether the Fool's relentless harping drives Lear mad. Most prefer to believe that the Fool serves a positive function when he criticises his master. He pushes Lear towards the truth and then tries to 'out-jest' his injuries, supporting the king as he makes his terrible journey through Act III. So why does the Fool disappear? Some commentators suggest Jacobean audiences would not have been disconcerted by the disappearance of a character half way through the play. Other critics think that the Fool is dropped when he is no longer needed. The Fool's role was to help Lear see more clearly and when his job is completed, he vanishes. Other critics suggest it would be inappropriate to have a comic character (however dark his humour) in the bleak final acts of the play. Finally, it is possible that the same actor played the Fool and Cordelia, and therefore they could not be on stage at the same time.

During this century, the interpretation and presentation of the Fool have become increasingly important to critics and directors. He has been played by women (though not always as female), as a music hall clown, as a waif in ragged clothes, as a worn out old man, as a young drag queen. In each case, the director seems to be choosing to emphasise a particular aspect of the relationship between Lear and his Fool, and something of his or her vision of the world of *King Lear*. Which version of the Fool do you feel adds most to your understanding of King Lear, the man, and *King Lear*, the play?

 CHECK THE NET

This site, which is a Shakespeare Resource Centre, has useful and accessible short sections on historical and social contexts (e.g. Elizabethan England, The Globe) and a reading list: **www.bardweb. net**.

QUESTION

Compare and contrast the roles and functions of the Fool and Kent.

KENT

Kent's most notable characteristics are his loyalty and bluntness. It is the former that motivates him and the latter which causes him trouble. Kent speaks up immediately when he sees Lear acting with 'hideous rashness' (I.1.151). He only resorts to blunt language – 'What wouldst thou do, old man?' (I.1.145) – when his respectful interjections are ignored. Thereafter he reverts to his usual reverence, addressing Lear as 'my lord' and 'my liege'. His dogged determination to stick to the 'old language' of Lear's court can be seen as a measure of his loyalty. It might also indicate that Kent is a conservative, backward-looking figure. There is other evidence that points in this direction. During Lear's madness Kent is reluctant to allow Poor Tom to accompany his master, failing to recognise the beggar's suffering and appalled that the king has 'no better company' (III.4.135). Is this moral blindness? Kent is a representative of the hierarchy that Lear destroyed when he gave away his power, an anachronism. It does not come as a surprise to hear him say he expects and hopes to die in Act V Scene 3. The world has moved on and Kent has no place in it now.

Does this seem harsh? Most critics would suggest that Kent is a wholly positive figure. His judgement and advice in Act I Scene 1 are absolutely sound, and his warnings are all justified by the events of the play. We can trust him. Kent accepts banishment without a grudge and immediately assumes a disguise so that he can continue to follow Lear. He suffers punishment stoically in Act II. Out in the storm he thinks only of his master's comfort. He is constantly active in Lear's service. His faithful perseverance is admirable. We can also admire Kent's anger because it always seems justified. Some critics argue that Kent's anger mars Lear's cause, but it is a relief to see a character take on Gonerill, Regan, Cornwall and Oswald. Kent voices the audience's concerns and opinions when he says: 'I have seen better faces in my time / Than stands on any shoulder that I see / Before me at this instant' (II.2.91–3).

Kent keeps us informed about important developments in the plot and acts as Cordelia's champion. However, in spite of his constancy, he begins to seem worn down in the second half of the play. He endures as long as his master needs him but his tone becomes increasingly melancholy when Cordelia reappears. His rhyming couplet at the end of Act IV Scene 7 is downbeat: 'My point and period will be throughly wrought / Or well or ill, as this day's battle's fought' (IV.7.96–7). Perhaps Shakespeare is using Kent to hint at Lear's death. Does Kent see that he will not be needed for much longer? Kent's lines in V.3 are weary too. His heavily **alliterated** description of Gonerill and Regan's deaths is like a bell tolling for Lear. Kent then comments sorrowfully on his master's passing, 'Vex not his ghost. O, let him pass. He hates him / That would upon the rack of this tough world / Stretch him out longer' (V.3.311–13). It is appropriate that the dependable Kent sums up his master's pain in this distressing scene. He can usually be relied on to hit the right note and will be seen by most audiences of most productions as a reliable guide to the characters and moods of the play. The world of *King Lear* would be considerably darker without Kent's diligence.

ALBANY AND CORNWALL

It is hard to judge the characters of Albany and Cornwall when they first appear on stage. They do not play any real part in the first scene, appearing only as consorts to their wives, Gonerill and Regan. Perhaps Shakespeare gives us a hint that Albany is to be trusted in the opening lines of the play when Kent tells us that Lear seems to favour him, but our attention is not focused on these two characters until later.

Albany can seem problematic. The audience is suspicious of Gonerill long before her husband recognises her inhumanity, and his interjections in the first scene in which he plays any significant part (Act I Scene 4) seem weak. Admittedly, he has missed much of Gonerill's hectoring of Lear, but 'What's the matter, sir?' (I.4.292) is surely inadequate. Are we to assume that Albany is so good himself that he has been taken in by Gonerill? After Lear takes himself off in high dudgeon, Albany wants to wait and see what happens. At this stage he certainly lacks Gonerill's force and decisiveness. It is easy to be critical of Albany's inaction and lack of foresight, but they are both necessary to the plot. If he attempted to check his wife's progress now, it would distract from the main business of the play at this point – Lear's deteriorating relationship with his daughters.

 CHECK THE NET
www.talkingto.co .uk/ttws – 'Talking to William Shakespeare'. This is an excellent site with a large number (50+) of questions and answers specifically on the play. Questions are provided by students and other interested readers, answers provided by scholars. Many of the questions are exactly the kind of questions that A-level students seek answers to when they are working on assignments. It is very accessible and the format of the site makes it very easy to use.

Albany's rectitude also contrasts neatly with Cornwall's increasing ruthlessness. In Act II Scene 1 we see how Regan's unpleasant husband is drawn to Edmund ('Natures of such deep trust we shall much need; / You we first seize on' – lines 114–15). This is a sure sign that Cornwall is morally dubious. We also quickly realise that unlike Albany, Cornwall is ready to assume command and join his wife and sister-in-law in their campaign against Lear. His tone is habitually authoritarian. He conducts the investigation into Kent and Oswald's altercation, and announces Kent's punishment in an angry tone that suggests 'the fiery quality of the Duke' (II.4.88). In Act III Scene 7 Cornwall's contempt for any authority other than his own is made horribly clear. He aspires to the crown and acts as if he were the law. Cornwall is responsible for the most shocking act of physical violence in *King Lear* – the blinding of Gloucester. This makes him utterly repugnant.

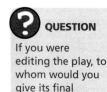

QUESTION

If you were editing the play, to whom would you give its final speech: Edgar or Albany? Why?

Having demonstrated the vile depths that humanity can sink to, Shakespeare has no further need of Cornwall. His death at the end of Act III enables Shakespeare to set up the sisters' rivalry for Edmund more effectively, and there is also the point made by the way Cornwall meets his end. His own servant turns on him, just as he turned on his host and his king. This is **poetic justice**. Cornwall's corruption is counterbalanced by his brother-in-law's increasing moral strength. Albany is absent from the play for two acts, and speaks with a new energy and decisiveness when he reappears. He also appears to have altered his opinion of his wife quite radically. His abuse of Gonerill when he accuses her of mistreating Lear indicates that we can now trust Albany (Act IV Scene 2). What we need from him, however, is action, not words. Albany rises to the occasion in Act V Scene 3. He denounces and arrests Edmund, offers to challenge him and then presides over the duel between Gloucester's two sons. After the fight, he continues to play an authoritarian role. He asks Edgar to tell the story of his miserable existence in hiding, enabling the audience to hear of Gloucester's death. It is also Albany who delivers a stern epitaph for Gonerill and Regan. Shakespeare now wants us to see him as an agent of justice and correct morality. When Lear appears Albany gracefully resigns the 'absolute power' he has briefly assumed as leader of the British forces. But his virtue is hopeless now. In the final moments of the play his words seem inadequate again. Albany's brief final lines suggest that language cannot express the distress and pity the characters feel at the end of the play.

Edgar's last speech is attributed to Albany in the Quarto, reinforcing his authority. But it remains difficult to believe in Albany. He is always too late, so often a bystander. One line in particular seems to undermine his good intentions completely. As Cordelia's body is carried on to the stage he calls out in alarm, 'The gods defend her' (V.3.254). We are forced to conclude that Albany is out of his depth in the world of *King Lear*.

OSWALD

Oswald is a minor character but he serves a number of useful functions. His most important role is as Gonerill's servant. He carries out orders diligently and faithfully and delivers a number of significant letters that move the action of the play on. He is Gonerill's agent in corruption and his bad qualities mirror his mistress's warped nature. Oswald is an insolent, cowardly liar and as self-seeking as the other evil characters. Keen to receive a financial reward, he is only too ready to kill Gloucester when he comes across him in Act IV. His selfish opportunism reflects Gonerill's ambitious rapacity. Oswald also provides a parallel with Kent (the honest plain-speaking servant) and awakens Edgar's valour.

IMAGES AND THEMES

These two aspects of the play are covered in the same section, since ideas are often developed through the patterns of images Shakespeare creates. Through a consideration of the **imagery** you will come to a fuller understanding of the play and its meanings. One of the most intriguing and rewarding aspects of studying *King Lear* is the fact that some of the images and themes remain perplexing. These notes are not exhaustive, and you will find it useful to work through the play yourself, tracing the development of images and considering your own responses to them.

 CHECK THE NET
For images, photos and paintings of Lear and links to other sites that include images visit **www.utdallas.edu /~kmarshal/ Shakespeare/lear. htm**.

CHECK THE NET

www.pathguy. com/KingLear is a good study site on the play; it includes comments on images and themes – particularly useful on the theme of nature and the word 'nothing'. There is also access to Tate's reworked version of the play from this site.

NOTHING

'Nothing' and 'Nothingness' are important concepts in *King Lear*. As he loses everything – his status, his family, his mind – Lear learns the value of Cordelia's 'Nothing, my lord' (I.1.87). Her refusal to participate in the love-test sets off the whole disastrous chain of events. Thereafter, other characters help Lear to come to terms with his 'nothingness', using **imagery** that echoes Cordelia's words. In Act I Scene 4 the Fool taunts Lear with the word 'nothing' (I.4.129–33 and I.4.187–90), and then in Act III the sight of Poor Tom pushes Lear to ask 'Is man no more than this?' (III.4.99–100). Finally Lear learns how empty Gonerill and Regan's words were and finds he has moved closer to Cordelia's true values: 'I know not what to say' he murmurs (IV.7.54).

'Nothing' causes Gloucester the same trouble in the subplot. Like Gonerill and Regan, Edmund uses false words to gain everything. Edmund pretends that his fake letter is 'Nothing, my lord', copying Cordelia's reply in an ironic and alarming way (I.2.32). Gloucester too loses everything, and learns to see more clearly. A very troublesome word, 'nothing'.

CLOTHING

CONTEXT

Metaphors of clothing are used throughout Shakespeare's plays, especially when the dramatist is interested in exploring ideas about appearance and reality.

References to clothing are closely linked to ideas about appearance and reality. Outward appearances are often deceptive in *King Lear*. When Lear stoops to blind folly it seems that honesty has to hide itself. Virtuous characters assume disguises in order to survive, continuing to do good in their new lowly roles. The apparel of Lear's closest companions on the heath – the Fool, Kent and Edgar – is significant. All three are humbly dressed; the Fool in his motley, Kent as a man servant and Edgar in the garb of the social outcast. In spite of their inferior status – signified by their clothing – servants are frequently the source of hope, charity and justice in *King Lear*.

Ceremonial garments and the clothing of the court are deeply suspect. They conceal the truth. Lear cannot see beyond the trappings of majesty and assumes his crown makes him 'ague-proof' (IV.6.104–5). Gonerill, Regan and Edmund cover up their depravity with attractive exteriors. When Lear is forced to face reality he decides to remove his kingly garments, 'Off off! You lendings' (III.4.105). His clothing is proof of his folly and inappropriate, for two reasons. Firstly, Lear no longer has any power, and secondly, he has started to look beyond appearances. He needs to rid himself of the trappings of majesty so that he can learn. In Act IV we know that Lear has gained wisdom when he says astutely 'furred gowns hide all' (IV.6.166). He has recognised the truth about himself and his daughters. When his sanity is restored Lear is ready to be put in fresh clothes. He no longer needs his crown of poisonous and bitter weeds, a symbol of his jarred senses. Appropriately, it is Cordelia – his truthful daughter – who instructs her servants to dress Lear in more fitting garments.

There are other references to clothing that help us understand the play. Like Poor Tom, Edgar warns against vanity, 'set not thy sweet heart on proud array' (III.4.79). Lear would have done well to heed this advice early in the play. Edgar also creates a history for Poor Tom as a lustful serving man who had 'three suits to his back, six shirts to his body' (III.4.129–30), linking clothing with corruption.

ANIMALS

There is a wealth of animal imagery in *King Lear*. The most important recurring references are to savage creatures, which are associated with Gonerill and Regan. The sisters are also likened to fiends and monsters. Gonerill is 'sharp-toothed, like a vulture', with a 'wolfish visage' (I.5.305). Lear curses her as a 'detested kite' (I.4.259) and tells Regan she 'looked black … most serpent like' upon him (I.4.156–7). Gloucester says the sisters possess 'boarish fangs' (III.7.57) and Albany eventually sees them as 'Tigers not daughters' (IV.2.40), who behave like 'monsters of the deep' (IV.2.49). Even Edmund, who is presumably attracted to the sisters, and described himself as a 'toad-spotted traitor', speaks of them using animal imagery (V.3.136). They are jealous as 'the stung / Are of the adder' (V.1.56–7). Their sexuality is as abhorrent as their cruelty. Lear describes women as living 'centaurs' (IV.6.124). The implications of all these references are clear: Gonerill and Regan are cruel predators, 'pelican daughters' who want to see their father bleed (III.4.72). Their inhumanity is reconfirmed when Gloucester and Cordelia describe how a wild beast would have been allowed

> **CONTEXT**
>
> When Lear addresses Edgar as a learned Theban and wise philosopher, we are given a glimpse of the importance of classical literature to Renaissance writers and thinkers. During the period that Shakespeare was writing, there had been a rediscovery of classical literature, largely through Roman texts.

shelter in the storm, but not Lear (III.7.61–4 and IV.7.36–40). Appropriately, Gonerill and Regan are destroyed by their animal instincts.

There are other references to animals which help us understand Lear's plight. The Fool uses telling imagery when he says to Lear 'the hedge-sparrow fed the cuckoo so long / That its had it head bit off by it young' (I.4.211–12). The image of Lear as a hedge-sparrow emphasises his vulnerability. Like Poor Tom, Edgar dwells on the way he is stalked by devils, recalling the way Lear is treated by Gonerill and Regan. Reduced to an abject state on the heath, Lear recognises that man is 'a poor bare forked animal' (III.4.104). His identification with Poor Tom again suggests Lear's helplessness. How could a 'poor bare forked animal' cope with the powerful predators linked to Gonerill and Regan? Lear's vulnerability is emphasised at the start of the final scene when the king pictures life in prison, where he and Cordelia will 'sing like birds in a cage' (V.3.9). For the first time we are presented with an attractive animal image. However, song-birds are passive, tame creatures. This image hints that Lear's visions of happiness are deluded.

SIGHT AND BLINDNESS

The importance of seeing yourself and the world clearly is one of the key themes in *King Lear*. It is reflected in the many images of sight and blindness, light and dark, eyes and weeping. One of the earliest references to eyes comes in Act I Scene 1, after Lear has explained his 'darker purpose' (I.1.36) and failed to see the truth about his three daughters. Kent tries to warn the king that he is behaving foolishly, 'see better, Lear' (I.1.158). He begs his master to let him remain 'The true blank of thine eye' (I.1.159). His reward is an angry dismissal, 'Out of my sight' (I.1.157). Unable to see anyone's merits or faults clearly, Lear refuses to look on those who have offended him. However, Lear has another critic who forces him to consider his actions more closely. The Fool sums up Lear's folly neatly with a **metaphor**, 'So out went the candle and we were left darkling' (I.4.213). This line serves as a prediction for the end of Act II, when Lear is overwhelmed by dark thoughts and shut out in the storm. We might also see Lear as the candle. As monarch he is the source of light and life in the kingdom. When he burns 'out' (is out of favour) all the characters associated with Lear are 'left darkling'.

After the storm, Lear's ability to see more clearly is apparent when he meets Gloucester. In IV.6 the black humour of the references to sight heightens the **pathos** of the old men's suffering. But it also comes as something of a relief. There is reason in Lear's madness now:

> LEAR: No eyes in your head, nor no money in your purse? Your eyes are in a heavy case, your purse in a light; yet you see how this world goes.
>
> GLOUCESTER: I see it feelingly
>
> LEAR: What, art mad? A man may see how this world goes with no eyes. Look with thine ears.   (IV.6.146–52)

Some critics find Lear's puns about eyes desperately cruel. But Gloucester and Lear do now 'see how the world goes'. They both 'stumbled' when they saw. Gloucester's blinding is the physical manifestation of the mental torture Lear endured on the heath. We were prepared for it by a series references to sight, which built up tension effectively. In Act I Scene 2 Gloucester asked Edmund to 'look into' Edgar's treachery and then in Act III Scene 7 the references to eyes come thick and fast, starting with Gonerill's 'Pluck out his eyes!' (III.7.5).

Until Cordelia returns, like Gloucester, we feel that all is 'dark and comfortless' (III.7.84). Cordelia is associated with healing tears and radiant light. Throughout his confrontations with Gonerill and Regan and during his descent into madness Lear refused to weep. 'Old fond eyes … I'll pluck ye out' he declared vehemently (I.4.298–9). His desperate struggle against weeping can be seen as proof of Lear's determination not to be vanquished by his pelican daughters. However, he cries when he is reunited with Cordelia. Is this a sign of weakness or an indication that he sees himself and his daughter more clearly? In Act V Lear is defiant again: he and Cordelia will not weep in prison. When she is hanged, Lear finally gives in to his grief, 'Howl, howl, howl! / O, you are men of stones! / Had I your tongues and eyes I'd use them so / That heaven's vault

CHECK THE NET

This is a comprehensive site which covers a lot of different materials and ideas about the play, particularly useful for students who want to read a detailed analysis of anger in the play, and a discussion of kingship. It also includes helpful study questions for students: **www. webenglish teacher.com/ kinglear.html**.

should crack' (V.3.255–7). His eyes fail him as he mourns the loss of his 'best object' (I.1.214).

MADNESS

Unlike other Renaissance dramatists, who used 'mad scenes' for comic effect, Shakespeare seems intent on a serious portrayal of madness in *King Lear*. There are different types of madness in the play. Lear's rash actions of Act I Scene 1 might be viewed as political insanity. The bloodlust exhibited by Gonerill, Regan and Cornwall is another abhorrent kind of madness. So how are we to view the king's descent into madness? Does insanity cure Lear's moral blindness? Lear compares his madness to the torments of hell and struggles frantically to retain his wits, 'O let me not be mad, not mad, sweet heaven!' (I.5.43). The other characters are horrified by his loss of reason and try desperately to keep him sane. The storm – which reflects Lear's madness – is appallingly destructive, almost too much for man to endure. It is particularly difficult to see Lear's madness as beneficial in Act V Scene 3. Having regained his wits and judgement, Lear is tormented again when Cordelia dies. In his final moments he is deluded once more, believing that his daughter still breathes.

There are other types of madness that shed a sombre light on Lear's insanity: the Fool's professional madness (his clowning), Edgar's fake madness and Gloucester's half-crazed pity. The madness of the Fool and Edgar might be intended to provide comic relief. The Fool's jests often lighten the tone and some of Edgar's antics as Poor Tom can seem amusing. The Elizabethans visited Bedlam (Bethlehem) Hospital for entertainment, to enjoy the spectacle of the mad beggars, so it is possible that Shakespeare intended the audience to laugh at Poor Tom. However, Edgar's craziness also seems designed to heighten the **pathos** of Act III; certainly, his descriptions of being driven close to suicide by devils are anything but funny. The same is true of the craziest scene in the play, the mock trial, which can be very disturbing on stage. Ultimately, the madness of *King Lear* is deeply distressing. It develops from and points back to the king's instability.

CONTEXT

According to the philosopher Aristotle, horror and pity are the two emotions that the audience should feel while watching a tragedy.

SUFFERING

The suffering in *King Lear* is intense, violent and relentless. Many of the characters are driven almost beyond the limits of endurance, reflected in the **imagery** of the play. Lear speaks of his daughters – especially Gonerill – attacking him physically. He tells Regan that her sister has 'struck' (II.4.155) him with her tongue and 'tied/Sharp-tooth'd unkindness' (II.4.129–30) around his heart. His daughters are 'a disease that's in my flesh ... a boil / A plague-sore, or embossed carbuncle, / In my corrupted blood' (II.4.216–20). Gonerill and Regan have wounded Lear and now eat away at his flesh. His 'frame of nature' is 'wrenched' from 'the fixed place' (I.4.265–6). As Lear's heart breaks 'into a hundred thousand flaws' his mind disintegrates (II.4.280). He is 'bound / Upon a wheel of fire', 'scalded' by his own tears (IV.7.45–8). Lear also employs images of the torments of hell when he rages against female sexuality in Act IV Scene 6. Femininity is closely linked to suffering in this play. Even when his senses are restored Lear continues to suffer. He has been 'cut to the brains' and finds it impossible to recover from his daughters' assault (IV.6.194). 'Burning shame' keeps him from Cordelia (IV.3.46). Guilt about his former unkindness stings his mind so 'venomously' that he cannot face her (IV.3.46).

The imagery that other characters use when commenting on Lear's pain echoes the king's words. Gloucester describes Lear as 'O ruined piece of nature!' (IV.6.135), for Edgar he is a 'side-piercing sight' (IV.6.85). The violence of so many of Edgar's frantic speeches as Poor Tom intensifies the sense of suffering on the heath. 'The foul fiend bites my back' (III.6.17) he wails, telling horrifying stories of being whipped, of knives in his bed and nooses on his balcony. Gloucester and Lear are overwhelmed by their suffering, in spite of their companions' efforts to alleviate their woes. Gloucester dies of a broken heart, while Lear's moment of greatest agony comes when Cordelia dies. He seems to choke to death, asking for a button to be unfastened. By now Kent welcomes death too. His line 'Break heart, I prithee break' might refer to Lear's suffering or his own (V.3.310). It is appropriate to both characters.

CHECK THE BOOK

For a bleak, existentialist reading of the view of humanity portrayed in the play, see Jan Kott, *Shakespeare Our Contemporary*, 1964.

At this point we need to consider what causes the intense suffering in *King Lear*. Gloucester thinks that the gods are sadistic, while Lear wants to know why nature has given him two malignant daughters. However, it is hard to blame the gods or nature for the violence in the play. The audience might feel that all the agony experienced can be traced back to human acts of unkindness. Characters suffer for their own sins or because they are sinned against. This seems harsh on the innocents, Cordelia and Edgar, but Gloucester and Lear hardly deserve the extreme torment they endure either. And it is not only the characters who suffer. At the end of the play the state is in disarray, signified by the word 'gored' (V.3.318). The storm serves as a **metaphor** for England's suffering as well as Lear's. The worst torments in *King Lear* are caused and perpetuated by the characters themselves.

But what is learned through suffering? Our understanding of the suffering in the play needs to include an assessment of its benefits. The good endure and help each other. Lear and Gloucester become more compassionate, reassessing themselves and the society they live in. Edgar becomes stronger and fit to rule. Through suffering these three male characters achieve heroism. It seems that the best natures can absorb pain and learn. In *King Lear* Shakespeare seems to suggest that it is man's fate to suffer. Lear says this very plainly in Act IV, 'When we are born we cry that we are come / To this great stage of fools' (IV.6.183–4).

NATURE

On the heath Lear tries to find answers to two questions. Why do his daughters have such hard hearts and what is the cause of thunder? His assumptions about what is natural have been challenged. He wants to know whether nature is responsible for his turmoil. The play does not provide straightforward answers to Lear's queries. We are presented with conflicting views of nature and what is natural. The dominance of the evil characters might lead us to feel that nature is a cruel force in *King Lear*. Edmund suggests that nature is a malevolent goddess who provides him with the bad nature necessary to challenge the status quo. Therefore his badness is natural. Gonerill and Regan's careers seem to confirm Edmund's view. Cruelty comes naturally to them and they delight in it. For these characters there is no natural order; they seek to create their own selfish universe.

But the good characters see this trio as unnatural. We are told that Gonerill and Regan behave monstrously, in a way that shames nature. So there is another kind of nature to consider: benign nature. Cordelia calls on the 'unpublished virtues of the earth' to restore Lear and displays the virtues of a good nature (IV.4.16). For Kent, the Fool, Edgar and Cordelia it is natural to be loving, trusting and loyal. Watching these characters it is possible to conclude that human nature is good. This group also believes in a natural order, which they struggle to restore. Yet they suffer.

We need to look to Lear for answers to these puzzles. The king represents the natural order. At the start of the play he presides over a harmonious hierarchy. Lear transgresses against the natural order when he fails to recognise Cordelia's worthiness, falsely calling her 'a wretch whom nature is ashamed / Almost t' acknowledge hers' (I.1.212–13). He compounds his mistake when he gives Gonerill and Regan power over him. Lear's unnatural dealing leads to unnatural dealing in others. Gloucester errs in a similar fashion, disinheriting his legitimate heir in favour of the bastard, whom he mistakes for a 'Loyal and natural boy' (II.1.83). Lear and Gloucester's errors are disastrous. Lear finds that his 'frame of nature' has been wrenched 'From the fixed place' (I.4.265–6). This image suggests the seriousness of Lear's crimes against the natural order. An enormous struggle ensues, as nature tries to reassert herself. The storm can be seen as both punishment and protest.

And yet, at the close of Act V, it is difficult to believe that nature is benevolent or that the natural order has really 'won'. Cordelia's death presents a problem for those who wish to see the end of *King Lear* as a triumph for nature and the hierarchy. Lear seems to suggest that nature is barbaric when he asks, 'Why should a dog, a horse, a rat have life, / And thou no breath at all?' (V.3.304–5). Perhaps we are meant to see Cordelia's death as the final punishment for Lear's transgression against nature. And Edgar may be a worthy monarch in the making, but his succession is hardly a triumph for the natural order.

 CHECK THE BOOK

For a detailed discussion of Nature in the play, see Kiernan Ryan, *Shakespeare: Texts and Contexts*, 2000.

Do we have answers to Lear's questions? We probably accept that Gonerill and Regan are naturally evil. There is no obvious reason why they have hard hearts. But it is Lear who causes the thunder; he allows the hard hearts a free reign. Our conclusion must be that nature reflects the mistakes of man in *King Lear*. And when man stoops to folly, the natural order is easily destroyed.

JUSTICE

Throughout *King Lear* characters judge and put each other on trial. Gloucester and Lear both misjudge their children, who seem to possess better judgement. Cordelia has the measure of her sisters and Gonerill and Regan's assessment of their father is acute and accurate. Edmund knows exactly how to take in his gullible relatives. It seems that good judgement is not the preserve of those with good intentions.

The workings of human justice reflect Lear and Gloucester's faults. The 'trials' that occur in the play are all flawed. Lear's 'love-test' is ill-conceived and has disastrous consequences. In Act II the trial of Kent for plain-speaking is an excuse for Cornwall and Regan to exercise power in an arrogant way. Lear's mock trial of Gonerill and Regan is presided over by a lunatic and attended by a fake madman and a court jester. The defendant is a joint-stool. This trial is a parody of the love-test. It highlights the absurdity of Lear's actions in Act I Scene 1. It also undermines all the other trials carried out by authority figures in *King Lear*. Gloucester's blinding is an appalling example of human injustice. Cornwall and Regan pervert the law to satisfy their own craving for revenge. It is possible to see the battle between the French and English forces as another trial which has dire consequences. Cordelia is hanged in prison and Lear dies. Some see Cordelia's death as the greatest injustice in the play. Human judgement and the justice system look extremely fallible when the curtain goes down on Act V.

QUESTION

How far do you agree that there is no justice in the play?

This point is reinforced by the examples of natural or **poetic justice** that we see in the play. In Act V Scene 3 Edgar takes the law into his own hands when he challenges Edmund. This is 'wild justice' at work. However, we accept the outcome of the duel as appropriate. Edmund deserves to die. We see poetic justice at work elsewhere;

Cornwall is turned on and killed by his own servant, Gonerill and Regan are destroyed by their jealous lust and Oswald meets a sticky end.

The thorniest question about justice concerns Gloucester and Lear. Do they deserve to suffer and die? Some critics would say that a rather harsh kind of justice is at work here. Edgar suggests this when he says to Edmund, 'The dark and vicious place where thee he got / Cost him his eyes' (V.3.170–1). Gloucester pays very dearly for his sins (although some Elizabethans believed that blinding was the appropriate punishment for adultery). Lear also pays for his sins. Cordelia is taken from him immediately after he recognises her merits. Although his judgement has been restored, it is too late for Lear.

King Lear is also concerned with social justice. Lear and Gloucester both consider this topic carefully and seem to reach radical conclusions. Gloucester calls on the heavens to distribute wealth more evenly, while Lear considers the lives of the 'Poor naked wretches' he paid so little attention to (III.4.28–36). In Act IV Lear rages against corrupt members of the judiciary and seems to sneer at himself and all those who presume to rule and judge others when he says, 'a dog's obeyed in office' (IV.6.159–60).

 CHECK THE NET
For images & paintings of Lear see **www.uaf.edu/ english/faculty/ta/ gaskin/lear/links**.

At the end of the play we are presented with two new agents of justice, Albany and Edgar. We accept the justice of their actions in Act V Scene 3. But human judgement still looks faulty. Albany has almost been overwhelmed by events and Edgar's bitter words about Gloucester's death seem callous. Surely no one in *King Lear* is morally impeccable? Perhaps Shakespeare wants us to remain uncomfortable about justice.

THE GODS

There are many references to the pagan and Christian deities in *King Lear*. The characters appeal to them in times of crisis, hoping for divine assistance. Their attitudes towards the gods reflect their natures. Ideas about the gods can also be linked to the theme of justice. Are the gods just, indifferent or destructive? We hear conflicting views from the characters. At the start of the play Lear

believes that the gods are on his side. He expects them to punish
Gonerill and Regan for their ingratitude. Later, however, Lear
worries that the heavens are hostile; perhaps they stir 'these
daughters' hearts / Against their father' (II.4.269–70). His paranoia
reflects his egotism and instability. By Act V he seems to have
rediscovered his faith. We see the strength of Lear's love when he
says it will take 'a brand from heaven' to part him and Cordelia
(V.3.23). There is a terrible irony in the fact that it is a mere mortal,
Edmund, who deprives Lear of his beloved daughter. Lear makes no
mention of the gods when he asks why Cordelia has been killed.
His silence might be read as proof that we are to blame man for the
carnage of Act V.

**CHECK
THE BOOK**

For a reading of the
play which offers an
unchristian concept
of the gods, see
William Empson's
*Essays on
Shakespeare*, 1986.

Other characters' attitudes to the gods make the issue of faith
thornier still. What are we to make of Cordelia and Edgar, who
behave with Christian fortitude and the virtues of patience, pity and
benevolence? The religious imagery used to describe Cordelia in
Act IV Scene 6 clearly identifies her as an example of Christian
goodness. Cordelia sees the gods as kindly and helpful, calling on
them to restore Lear's senses. But she is sacrificed. How can we
believe the gods are just when her body is carried on to the stage
directly after Albany's line 'The gods defend her' (V.3.254)? At this
moment we are likely to agree with Gloucester's pessimistic
assessment of the gods; they seem capricious and sadistic. Edgar's
faith presents problems too. His statement, 'The gods are just, and
of our pleasant vices / Make instruments to plague us' does not ring
true when Cordelia is hanged (V.3.168–9). It is hard to reconcile
Edgar's belief in the justice of divine retribution with his description
of his journey through the play as a 'pilgrimage' (V.3.194). And does
his father really deserve to die for adultery?

So, is Shakespeare making a case for atheism? Does Cordelia's death
undermine every positive statement made about the gods in *King
Lear*? We need to consider Edmund, who professes to worship
nature but shows little respect for any religion. When he does refer
to the gods Edmund speaks ironically. In Act II Scene 1 he mocks
his father when he pretends to believe in 'the revenging gods /
'Gainst parricides' (II.1.44–5). Even when he pants for life and
decides to do good in Act V Scene 3, Edmund never suggests that

his change of heart comes about because he suddenly believes in divine retribution. The alacrity of Edmund's rise and the fact that the faithless, worldly bastard is responsible for Cordelia's death suggest man is as powerful and cruel as any force above. However, Edmund's progress is eventually stopped by two god-fearing characters. The atheist is not allowed to defeat the faithful. Shakespeare refuses to provide us with any straightforward answers to the many questions we have about religion in *King Lear*.

THE FAMILY AND FEUDALISM

The Jacobean age was a time of social and religious change. The feudal, medieval view of the world was under scrutiny and traditional assumptions about gender and class were being questioned by many. With its focus on the king and his family, many contemporary critics believe that *King Lear* reflects the anxieties of the period. The play charts the breakdown – not just of a character – but of a whole way of life. Albany and Kent's opening lines hint that we are in a world of political uncertainty.

In Act I Scene 1 Lear behaves like a medieval monarch. He is used to wielding his power with absolute authority and expects meek obedience. When Kent challenges him he is outraged, 'On thine allegiance' he rages (I.1.167). He dismisses Cordelia with words which reflect his power, 'Better thou had not been born than not t' have pleased me better' (I.1.232–3), and 'begone / Without our grace, our love, our benison!' (I.2.264–5). When she is disinherited Cordelia becomes a nonentity. She can only regain a position in the world when she is chosen in marriage by another man, who takes her without that symbol of her father's power, her dowry. Lear's medieval absolutism is already being undermined.

When he rejects Cordelia, Lear plunges his family and community into crisis. He allows a new breed of opportunists to undermine the hierarchy. It is a measure of the strength of the new breed that they get as far as they do. Gonerill, Regan and Edmund will not accept the roles allotted to them. Gonerill and Regan refuse to behave like good, submissive Renaissance women should. Edmund will not be marginalised. All three grasp at and enjoy exercising power. They show no respect for the family or the state. Even when Gonerill,

CONTEXT
Renaissance society was patriarchal and gerontocratic; men did not consider retirement, nor did they pass on their power and wealth when they reached old age. They retained their power until they died.

CONTEXT
The rituals that we see Lear trying to act out in Act I Scene 1 mirror the ceremonial public rituals that English culture demanded. Elizabeth I and James I expected their subjects to kneel, bow and scrape as marks of respect.

CHECK THE BOOK

For a discussion of feudalism in the play, see 'Shakespeare and the end of feudalism: *King Lear* as *fin-de-siecle* text' in *English Studies: A Journal of English Language and Literature*, vol. 78, no. 6, pp. 513–21.

Regan and Edmund are vanquished in Act V, the restored hierarchy looks shaky. The first family lies dead on the stage. The survivors are all numb, hardly ready to sustain the 'gored' state (V.3.228). Lear's family procession at the start of Act I was perhaps the final ceremony of an anachronistic code.

LANGUAGE

King Lear is written in **blank verse** and prose. Blank verse consists of unrhymed iambic pentameters, with five stressed syllables and five unstressed syllables to each line. You will notice that Shakespeare does not stick to the rules of blank verse rigidly. He uses shorter lines for emphasis (you will find many examples of this, especially during tense moments or scenes of chaos). Longer lines are used to avoid the comic sing-song or monotonous effect of repeated iambic pentameters. At the end of scenes Shakespeare sometimes uses rhyming couplets to provide a sense of closure. Rhyme is also used to draw attention to particular thoughts or ideas. The Fool's songs and proverbs are an example of this.

'Low' or comic characters generally speak in prose in Elizabethan and Jacobean drama. Traditionally, scenes of madness were also written in prose. Shakespeare obeys these conventions in *King Lear*, but you will notice that prose is used on other occasions too. Sometimes scenes contain both verse and prose. We would expect Lear to speak in verse because he is a king. However, as his wits desert him, he shifts from verse to prose and back again, signifying the disruption in his mind. You will also notice that Lear uses the third person (the royal 'we') early in the play, but adopts the more humble first person ('I', 'methinks') when he recognises that he is powerless. This change reflects his change in status, from king to 'a foolish old man'. You might want to consider the dramatic effects of other language choices. For example, why does Gloucester enter in Act I Scene 2 muttering in prose? Perhaps Shakespeare wants to show how troubled Gloucester is as he feverishly considers recent events. The swift moving prose also perhaps anticipates Gloucester's hasty decision-making later in the scene.

The language of *King Lear* – especially the final scene – is direct and simple, with the exception of Edgar's mad talk and the Fool's riddles. This simplicity is an integral part of the play's dramatic power, as are two other conventions. Characters use **asides** and **soliloquies** to inform the audience about their feelings and intentions, drawing us into their world. Characters also have their own personal 'styles', reflecting their roles, emotions and natures. For example, Gonerill and Regan use clipped commands, which demonstrate their craving for power. The patterns of **images** and **metaphors** Shakespeare uses add to our understanding of the play and its characters enormously and should be considered alongside style and punctuation in any analysis of Shakespeare's use of language in *King Lear* (see **Images and themes**).

CHECK THE BOOK

For a discussion of language and silence, see Gamini Salgado, *King Lear: Text and Performance*, 1993.

PART FOUR

CRITICAL HISTORY

King Lear has enjoyed a rich critical history. This section offers an overview of some of the ideas that have exercised the minds of writers and scholars over the past three centuries.

CONTEXT

The real King Leir lived 800 years BC, in a pagan era.

SEVENTEENTH-CENTURY CRITICISM

During Shakespeare's lifetime *King Lear* does not appear to have been as successful as *Hamlet* or *Macbeth*. We can presume the play was well received, however, because it was performed at court for James I. Thereafter, for the rest of the seventeenth century, it seems to have been ignored. After the Restoration, *King Lear* was rewritten by Nahum Tate in 1681. Tate felt that the ending was far too gloomy. He also felt that the structure of the play was disorganised. His version of *King Lear* includes a happy ending (Lear does not die) and a romance between Edgar and Cordelia.

EIGHTEENTH-CENTURY CRITICISM

Two noteworthy eighteenth-century critics agreed with Tate's assessment of *King Lear* as faulty. In 1753 Joseph Wharton objected to the Gloucester subplot as unlikely and distracting, and reckoned Gloucester's blinding too horrid to be exhibited on the stage. Wharton also found Gonerill and Regan's savagery too diabolical to be credible. While he accepted the way in which 'the wicked prosper and the virtuous miscarry' because it was 'a just representation of the common events of human life', Samuel Johnson (1768) took Shakespeare to task for the lack of justice at the end of *King Lear*. He found Cordelia's death deeply shocking. These early critics were on sound territory; scholars are still arguing about the savagery in *King Lear*, and whether or not justice exists in the world of the play.

NINETEENTH-CENTURY CRITICISM

Moving on to the nineteenth century, we find a range of views, although critics agreed that the play was harsh. Charles Lamb (1811) thought *King Lear* unactable. August Wilhelm Schlegel (1808) saw a drama in which 'the science of compassion is exhausted': 'humanity is stripped of all external and internal advantages, and given up prey to naked helplessness'. William Hazlitt (1817) noted the 'giddy anarchy' of *King Lear*, and the way in which the unnatural comes to dominate. However, Hazlitt also believed that Shakespeare showed a 'firm faith in filial piety'. Again, all these ideas have been taken up by contemporary critics; suffering, anarchy, bleakness, faith, and the topic that obsesses Lear so much – the behaviour of children.

At the end of the century the poet Swinburne (1880) was struck by the dark fatalism of Shakespeare's vision. 'Requital, redemption, amends, equity, pity and mercy are words without a meaning here'. Other Victorian critics saw grandeur and strength in the play, and Lear continued to trouble and move them. *King Lear* was now recognised as a great literary achievement. For George Brandes (1895), Cordelia was 'the living emblem of womanly dignity', while the play as a whole portrayed 'the titanic tragedy of human life; there rings forth from it a chorus of passionate jeering, wildly yearning, and desperate wailing voices'. The sense of despair Brandes identifies here continued to be important to twentieth-century critics.

EARLY TWENTIETH-CENTURY CRITICISM

There were many movements in literary criticism during the twentieth century, with each new discipline rejecting or reworking the ideas of previous critics. A range of conflicting views of *King Lear* emerged. A major development in Shakespearean criticism came with the publication of A.C. Bradley's *Shakespearean Tragedy* in 1905. Bradley believed that it was possible to understand a text and the playwright's intentions through close reading. He focused

CHECK THE BOOK

For a reading of the play as a Christian parable of sacrifice and salvation, see A.C. Bradley's *Shakespearean Tragedy*, 1992.

CHECK THE NET
This site has access to the Bradley material:
www.clicknotes. com/bradley.

on character and motivation. For Bradley a Shakespearean tragedy is the tragedy of an individual who suffers as he comes to terms with his personality. Bradley made many criticisms of *King Lear*, commenting on careless inconsistencies, the loose, episodic structure and the unwieldy subplot. However, he also conceded that the play was 'one of the world's greatest poems'. For him Lear was a great, superior figure, whose suffering is heart-rending. Bradley also felt that this solemn tragedy was essentially unfathomable. Although Bradley's emphasis on character has been rejected by recent critics, many would agree that *King Lear* remains impossible to pin down.

In 1930, G. Wilson Knight's *The Wheel of Fire* was published. In '*King Lear* and the Comedy of the Grotesque', Wilson Knight explored the absurd cruelty in the play. 'The tragedy is most poignant in that it is purposeless, unreasonable. It [*King Lear*] is the most fearless artistic facing of the ultimate cruelty of things in our literature. That cruelty would be less were there not this element of comedy … Mankind is, as it were, deliberately or comically tormented by "the gods". He is not even allowed to die tragically'. This view of the play marks a departure from previous accounts of *King Lear*. Up to now, there had been very little emphasis on the (horrible) comedy of the play, even though the cruelty and absurdity had been noted before.

The question of whether or not *King Lear* can be interpreted as a 'Christian play' has troubled many critics. Some see Cordelia as a Christ-like figure, who redeems Lear (thus his sufferings have not been in vain). Cordelia and Edgar's Christian virtues are commented upon and Lear too is recognised as displaying the virtue of patience. There are obvious problems with the Christian view, which fellow critics have been keen to point out. Why do the good characters' calls for justice from the gods go unheeded? Why does the ending feel so bleak? The agnostic view has tended to dominate. W.R. Elton (1966) refutes the Christian critics' positive readings of *King Lear*. He sees Cordelia's hanging and Gloucester's blinding as proof of 'the wilful operations of an upside down providence in an apparently deranged universe'. In his *Penguin Critical Studies: King Lear* (1986), Kenneth Muir, a **humanist** critic, agrees with Elton. 'In

CONTEXT
In November 1606, less than two months before *King Lear* was performed at court, James I opened Parliament with a speech urging a decision on the Union of Scotland and England, a project that preoccupied him during his early years on the English throne. He dearly hoped that the two countries could be united, but the English Parliament repeatedly thwarted his plans.

King Lear', Muir says, 'he [Shakespeare] starts from the hypothesis, whatever his personal beliefs, that the gods are indifferent, or hostile, or inexplicable, or even a man-made fiction, and that there is no after-life in which the injustices of life on earth may be set right. It follows that human beings are entirely responsible for their actions, and that if these lead to disaster, the tragedy is absolute'. After these pessimistic comments, however, Muir finds a reason to be more optimistic. He notes that many characters act with Christian morals, seeking to do good, regardless of the chaos that surrounds them. Thus, Shakespeare does not present man as completely evil.

www. **CHECK THE NET**
www.shakespeare
.palomar.edu –
'Mr William
Shakespeare and
the Internet' is an
excellent guide to
Shakespeare
resources on the
net and general
criticism in
particular.

CONTEMPORARY CRITICISM

More recently, scholars have become interested in the political and social implications of *King Lear*. Debate is focused on class, gender, race, the family, authority, the structures of power, and the meanings and functions of literary criticism itself. Some of the most interesting work on *King Lear* has come from **feminist** and **new historicist** critics.

NEW HISTORICISM

In *Radical Tragedy* (1984), Jonathan Dollimore completely reassesses *King Lear*. For him the play is not about the heroism of human endurance, or the moral growth of a hero who comes to know himself more thoroughly. Dollimore moves away from the analysis of character and individual suffering favoured by Bradley. He suggests that Lear's identity is a social construction; 'What makes Lear the person he is – or rather was – is not kingly essence (divine right), but, among other things, his authority and his family'. Lear loses his mind when he loses his social status. As the play progresses Lear is stripped of his 'conceptions of self'; he is forced to question his identity, 'Does any here know me?' … 'who is it that can tell me who I am?'

CHECK THE BOOK
For a new historicist
reading of the play,
see Stephen
Greenblatt's essay,
'The Cultivation of
Anxiety: King Lear
and his Heirs' in
*King Lear: A
Casebook*, ed.
Kiernan Ryan, 1993.

Dollimore believes *King Lear* is really about 'power, property and inheritance'. In this play Shakespeare focuses on what happens when there is 'a catastrophic redistribution of power'. Society is 'torn apart by conflict' because of its 'faulty ideological structure'. Looking at the end of Act V Scene 3 Dollimore sees a total collapse. Edgar and Albany try vainly to 'recuperate their society in just those terms the play is subjected to sceptical interrogation'. Thus, for Dollimore, *King Lear* is a subversive, radical **tragedy** which questions the Jacobean status quo.

Leonard Tennenhouse refutes Dollimore's subversive reading. For him *King Lear* shows us the opposite: the dangers of not following the 'old ways' of the patriarchal hierarchy. He sees the play as reconfirming oppressive structures, as being conservative in impulse. Tennenhouse would also deny that Shakespeare's portrayal of the sufferings of the poor and his concern with justice in *King Lear* are proof that the playwright viewed his society with a critical eye. However, other new historicist critics point to Lear's abuses of power as being direct comment on the vagaries of James I and his monarchy. In these readings, Shakespeare emerges as a social commentator.

FEMINIST CRITICISM

Feminist criticism of Lear incorporates a similar range of contrasting views. For Coppelia Kahn *King Lear* is a play about 'male anxiety'. Kahn suggests that Lear breaks down when he refuses to accept that he is dependent on his daughters, that he needs the feminine. Lear goes mad because he cannot face his feminine side; he refuses to cry. When Lear learns to weep, and rediscovers a loving non-patriarchal relationship with Cordelia, he is redeemed. In Kahn's view the play affirms femininity as a positive force.

 CHECK THE BOOK

For a feminist approach to the play, see Kathleen McCluskie's and Coppelia Kahn's essays in *King Lear: A Casebook*, ed. Kiernan Ryan, 1993.

Kathleen McCluskie's reading of *King Lear* asserts the opposite view. For her, Lear is an 'anti-feminine' play. She suggests 'the misogyny of King Lear, both the play and its hero, is constructed out of an ascetic tradition which presents women as the source of the primal sin of lust, combining with concerns about the threat to the family posed by female insubordination'. Her arguments are based on her recognition that the 'action of the play, the organisation of its points of view and the theatrical dynamic of its central scenes all depend upon an audience accepting an equation between "human nature" and "male power"'. McCluskie points out that the play forces us to sympathise with the patriarchs, Lear and Gloucester, and the masculine power structure they represent. She does not feel that Shakespeare presents a movement towards the feminine in *King Lear*, rather the reverse. 'Family relations in this play are seen as fixed and determined, and any movement within them is portrayed as a destructive reversal of the rightful order'. For McCluskie 'Cordelia's saving love, so much admired by critics, works … less as a redemption of womankind than as an example of patriarchy restored'. The audience is forced to agree that evil women (Gonerill and Regan) create a chaotic world, and must be resisted. The feminine must either be made to submit (Cordelia) or destroyed (Gonerill and Regan).

To explore these diverse ideas further it is best to consider your own response to the play and then return to the critics themselves in full. You will find some of the critics mentioned here in the books listed in **Further reading**.

CONTEXT

James I's views on challenging kings reflected Lear's; 'it is sedition in subjects to dispute what a king may do in the height of his powers.' Sounding uncannily like Lear, he also commented in 1610; 'I am now an old king… I must not be taught my office.'

PART FIVE

BACKGROUND

WILLIAM SHAKESPEARE'S LIFE

There are no personal records of Shakespeare's life. Official documents and occasional references to him by contemporary dramatists enable us to draw the main outline of his public life, but his private life remains hidden. Although not at all unusual for a writer of his time, this lack of first-hand evidence has tempted many to read his plays as personal records and to look in them for clues to Shakespeare's character and convictions. The results are unconvincing, partly because Renaissance art was not subjective or designed primarily to express its creator's personality, and partly because the drama of any period is very difficult to read biographically. Except when plays are written by committed dramatists to promote social or political causes (as by Shaw or Brecht), it is all but impossible to decide who amongst the variety of fictional characters in a drama represents the dramatist, or which of the various and often conflicting points of view expressed is authorial.

What we do know can be quickly summarised. Shakespeare was born into a well-to-do family in the market town of Stratford-upon-Avon in Warwickshire, where he was baptised, in Holy Trinity Church, on 26 April 1564. His father, John Shakespeare, was a prosperous glover and leather merchant who became a person of some importance in the town: in 1565 he was elected an alderman of the town, and in 1568 he became high bailiff (or mayor) of Stratford. In 1557 he had married Mary Arden. Their third child (of eight) and eldest son, William, learned to read and write at the primary (or 'petty') school in Stratford and then, it seems probable, attended the local grammar school, where he would have studied Latin, history, logic and rhetoric. In November 1582 William, then aged eighteen, married Anne Hathaway, who was twenty-six years old. They had a daughter, Susanna, in May 1583, and twins, Hamnet and Judith, in 1585.

CHECK THE BOOK

There are a number of biographies of Shakespeare – many of them very speculative – but the most authoritative is still Samuel Schoenbaum's *Shakespeare: A Documentary Life* (1975).

Shakespeare next appears in the historical record in 1592 when he is mentioned as a London actor and playwright in a pamphlet by the dramatist Robert Greene. These 'lost years' 1585–92 have been the subject of much speculation, but how they were occupied remains as much a mystery as when Shakespeare left Stratford, and why. In his pamphlet, *Greene's Groatsworth of Wit*, Greene expresses to his fellow dramatists his outrage that the 'upstart crow' Shakespeare has the impudence to believe he 'is as well able to bombast out a blank verse as the best of you'. To have aroused this hostility from a rival, Shakespeare must, by 1592, have been long enough in London to have made a name for himself as a playwright. We may conjecture that he had left Stratford in 1586 or 1587.

During the next twenty years, Shakespeare continued to live in London, regularly visiting his wife and family in Stratford. He continued to act, but his chief fame was as a dramatist. From 1594 he wrote exclusively for the Lord Chamberlain's Men, which rapidly became the leading dramatic company and from 1603 enjoyed the patronage of James I as the King's Men. His plays were extremely popular and he became a shareholder in his theatre company. He was able to buy lands around Stratford and a large house in the town, to which he retired about 1611. He died there on 23 April 1616 and was buried in Holy Trinity Church on 25 April.

CHECK THE NET
You can read Shakespeare's will in his own handwriting – and in modern transcription – online at the Public Records Office: **http://www.pro. gov.uk/ virtualmuseum** and search for 'Shakespeare'.

SHAKESPEARE'S DRAMATIC CAREER

Between the late 1580s and 1613 Shakespeare wrote thirty-seven plays, and contributed to some by other dramatists. This was by no means an exceptional number for a professional playwright of the times. The exact date of the composition of individual plays is a matter of debate –the date of first performance is known for only a few plays – but the broad outlines of Shakespeare's dramatic career have been established. He began in the late 1580s and early 1590s by rewriting earlier plays and working with plotlines inspired by the Classics. He concentrated on comedies (such as *The Comedy of Errors*, 1590–4, which derived from the Latin playwright Plautus) and plays dealing with English history (such as the three parts of *Henry VI*, 1589–92), though he also tried his hand at bloodthirsty revenge tragedy (*Titus Andronicus*, 1592–3, indebted to both Ovid and Seneca). During the 1590s Shakespeare developed his expertise

CHECK THE FILM

There are lots of anachronisms and inaccuracies in *Shakespeare in Love* (1998) – that's half the fun of it – but its depiction of the hand-to-mouth world of the commercial theatre has something of the energy and edginess from which Shakespeare drew his artistic power.

CONTEXT

A quarto is a small format book, roughly equivalent to a modern paperback. Play texts in quarto form typically cost sixpence, as opposed to the cost of going to the theatre at a penny.

in these kinds of plays to write comic masterpieces such as *A Midsummer Night's Dream* (1594–5) and *As You Like It* (1599–1600) and history plays such as *Henry IV* (1596–8) and *Henry V* (1598–9).

As the new century begins a new note is detectable. Plays such as *Troilus and Cressida* (1601–2) and *Measure for Measure* (1603–4), poised between comedy and tragedy, evoke complex responses. Because of their generic uncertainty and ambivalent tone such works are sometimes referred to as 'problem plays', but it is tragedy which comes to dominate the extraordinary sequence of masterpieces: *Hamlet* (1600–1), *Othello* (1602–4), *King Lear* (1605–6), *Macbeth* (1605–6) and *Antony and Cleopatra* (1606).

In the last years of his dramatic career, Shakespeare wrote a group of plays of a quite different kind. These 'romances', as they are often called, are in many ways the most remarkable of all his plays. The group comprises *Pericles* (1608), *Cymbeline* (1609–11), *The Winter's Tale* (1610–11) and *The Tempest* (1610–11). These plays (particularly *Cymbeline*) reprise many of the situations and themes of the earlier dramas but in fantastical and exotic dramatic designs which, set in distant lands, covering large tracts of time and involving music, mime, dance and tableaux, have something of the qualities of masques and pageants. The situations which in the tragedies had led to disaster are here resolved: the great theme is restoration and reconciliation. Where in the tragedies Ophelia, Desdemona and Cordelia die, the daughters of these plays – Marina, Imogen, Perdita, Miranda – survive and are reunited with their parents and lovers.

THE TEXTS OF SHAKESPEARE'S PLAYS

Nineteen of Shakespeare's plays were printed during his lifetime in what are called 'quartos': books, each containing one play, and made up of sheets of paper each folded twice to make four leaves. Shakespeare, however, did not supervise their publication. This was not unusual. When a playwright sold a play to a dramatic company he sold his rights in it: copyright belonged to whoever had possession of an actual copy of the text, and consequently authors had no control over what happened to their work. Anyone who could get hold of the text of a play might publish it if they wished. Hence, what found its way into print might be the author's copy, but it might be an actor's copy or prompt copy, perhaps cut or altered for performance; sometimes actors (or even members of the audience) might publish what they could remember of the text. Printers, working without the benefit of the author's oversight, introduced their own errors, through misreading the manuscript for example, and by 'correcting' what seemed to them not to make sense.

In 1623 John Heminges and Henry Condell, two actors in Shakespeare's company, collected together texts of thirty-six of Shakespeare's plays (*Pericles* was omitted) and published them in a large folio (a book in which each sheet of paper is folded once in half, to give two leaves). This, the First Folio, was followed by later editions in 1632, 1663 and 1685. Despite its appearance of authority, however, the texts in the First Folio still present many difficulties, for there are printing errors and confused passages in the plays, and its texts often differ significantly from those of the earlier quartos, when these exist.

Shakespeare's texts have, then, been through a number of intermediaries. We do not have the playwright's authority for any of his plays, and hence we cannot know exactly what it was that he wrote. Bibliographers, textual critics and editors have spent a great deal of effort on endeavouring to get behind the errors, uncertainties and contradictions in the available texts to recover the plays as Shakespeare originally wrote them. What we read is the result of these efforts. Modern texts are what editors have constructed from the available evidence: they correspond to no sixteenth- or seventeenth-century editions, and to no early performance of a Shakespeare play. Furthermore, these composite texts differ from each other, for different editors read the early texts differently and come to different conclusions. A Shakespeare text is an unstable and a contrived thing.

Often, of course, its judgements embody, if not the personal prejudices of the editor, then the cultural preferences of the time in which he or she was working. Growing awareness of this has led

 CHECK THE NET

You can find out more about the earliest editions of Shakespeare at the University of Pensylvannia's ERIC site: **http://oldsite. library.upenn.edu/ etext/collections/ furness/eric/eric. html**.

CONTEXT

King Lear was written during a time of uncertainty and unrest. In the year that the play was first performed, London had been decimated by the plague, which shut the theatres. In 1605 Guy Fawkes' plot to blow up Parliament and kill James I was foiled.

recent scholars to distrust the whole editorial enterprise and to repudiate the attempt to construct a 'perfect' text. Stanley Wells and Gary Taylor, the editors of the Oxford edition of *The Complete Works* (1988), point out that almost certainly the texts of Shakespeare's plays were altered in performance, and from one performance to another, so that there may never have been a single version. They note, too, that Shakespeare probably revised and rewrote some plays. They do not claim to print a definitive text of any play, but prefer what seems to them the 'more theatrical' version, and when there is a great difference between available versions, as with *King Lear*, they print two texts.

SHAKESPEARE AND THE ENGLISH RENAISSANCE

Shakespeare arrived in London at the very time that the Elizabethan period was poised to become the 'golden age' of English literature. Although Elizabeth reigned as queen from 1558 to 1603, the term 'Elizabethan' is used very loosely in a literary sense to refer to the period 1580 to 1625, when the great works of the age were produced. (Sometimes the later part of this period is distinguished as 'Jacobean', from the Latin form of the name of the king who succeeded Elizabeth, James I of England and VI of Scotland, who reigned from 1603 to 1625.) The poet Edmund Spenser heralded this new age with his pastoral poem *The Shepheardes Calender* (1579), and in his essay *An Apologie for Poetrie* (written about 1580, although not published until 1595) his friend Sir Philip Sidney championed the imaginative power of the 'speaking picture of poesy', famously declaring that 'Nature never set forth the earth in so rich a tapestry as divers poets have done ... Her world is brazen, the poet's only deliver a golden'.

www. **CHECK THE NET**

You can consult texts by Spenser and Sidney, and other contemporaries of Shakespeare , at Renascence Editions **http://www. uoregon.edu/ ~rbear/ren.htm**.

Spenser and Sidney were part of that rejuvenating movement in European culture which since the nineteenth century has been known by the term 'Renaissance'. Meaning literally 'rebirth' it denotes a revival and redirection of artistic and intellectual endeavour which began in Italy in the fourteenth century with the poetry of Petrarch. It spread gradually northwards across Europe, and is first detectable in England in the early sixteenth century in the writings of the scholar and statesman Sir Thomas More and in the poetry of Sir Thomas Wyatt and Henry Howard, Earl of Surrey. Its keynote was a curiosity in thought which challenged old assumptions and traditions. To the innovative spirit of the Renaissance, the preceding ages appeared dully unoriginal and conformist.

That spirit was fuelled by the rediscovery of many Classical texts and the culture of Greece and Rome. This fostered a confidence in human reason and in human potential which, in every sphere, challenged old convictions. The discovery of America and its peoples (Columbus had sailed in 1492) demonstrated that the world was a larger and stranger place than had been thought. The cosmological speculation of Copernicus (later confirmed by Galileo) that the sun, not the earth was the centre of our planetary system challenged the centuries-old belief that the earth and human beings were at the centre of the cosmos. The pragmatic political philosophy of Machiavelli seemed to cut politics free from its traditional link with morality by permitting to statesmen any means that secured the desired end. And the religious movements we know collectively as the Reformation broke with the Church of Rome and set the individual conscience, not ecclesiastical authority, at the centre of the religious life. Nothing, it seemed, was beyond questioning, nothing impossible.

Shakespeare's drama is innovative and challenging in exactly the way of the Renaissance. It examines and questions the beliefs, assumptions and politics upon which Elizabethan society was founded. And although the plays always conclude in a restoration of order and stability, many critics are inclined to argue that their imaginative energy goes into subverting, rather than reinforcing, traditional values. Frequently, figures of authority are undercut by some comic or parodic figure: against the Duke in *Measure for Measure* is set Lucio; against Prospero in *The Tempest*, Caliban; against Henry IV, Falstaff. Despairing, critical, dissident, disillusioned, unbalanced, rebellious, mocking voices are repeatedly to be heard in the plays, rejecting, resenting, defying the established order. They belong always to marginal, socially unacceptable figures, 'licensed', as it were, by their situations to say what would be unacceptable from socially privileged or responsible citizens. The

CHECK THE NET www.engl.uvic.ca/Faculty/MBHomePage/ISShakespeare/**Resources** for an essay on Renaissance views of madness in relation to Lear's plight by Adrian Ingham.

 CHECK THE NET The Luminarium site has links to a wide range of historical information on sixteenth-century topics including astronomy, medicine, economics and technology: **http://www.luminarium.org**.

question is: are such characters given these views to discredit them, or were they the only ones through whom a voice could be given to radical and dissident ideas? Was Shakespeare a conservative or a revolutionary?

Renaissance culture was intensely nationalistic. With the break-up of the internationalism of the Middle Ages the evolving nation states which still mark the map of Europe began for the first time to acquire distinctive cultural identities. There was intense rivalry among them as they sought to achieve, in their own vernacular languages, a culture that could equal that of Greece and Rome. Spenser's great allegorical epic poem *The Faerie Queene*, which began to appear from 1590, celebrated Elizabeth and was intended to outdo the poetic achievements of France and Italy and to stand beside the works of Virgil and Homer. Shakespeare is equally preoccupied with national identity. His history plays tell an epic story that examines how modern England came into being through the conflicts of the fifteenth-century Wars of the Roses which brought the Tudors to the throne. He is fascinated, too, by the related subject of politics and the exercise of power. With the collapse of medieval feudalism and the authority of local barons, the royal court in the Renaissance came to assume a new status as the centre of power and patronage. It was here that the destiny of a country was shaped. Courts, and how to succeed in them, consequently fascinated the Renaissance; and they fascinated Shakespeare and his audience.

But the dramatic gaze is not merely admiring; through a variety of devices, a critical perspective is brought to bear. The court may be paralleled by a very different world, revealing uncomfortable similarities (for example, Henry's court and the Boar's Head tavern, ruled over by Falstaff in *Henry IV*). Its hypocrisy may be bitterly denounced (for example, in the diatribes of the mad Lear) and its self-seeking ambition represented disturbingly in the figure of a Machiavellian villain (such as Edmund in *Lear*) or a malcontent (such as Iago in *Othello*). Shakespeare is fond of displacing the court to another context, the better to examine its assumptions and pretensions and to offer alternatives to the courtly life (for example, in the pastoral setting of the forest of Arden in *As You Like It* or

CHECK THE BOOK

Benedict Anderson's book on the rise of the nation and nationalism, *Imagined Communities* (revised ed., 1991), has been influential for its definition of the nation as 'an imagined political community' – imagined in part through cultural productions such as Shakespeare's history plays.

Prospero's island in *The Tempest*). Courtiers are frequently figures of fun whose unmanly sophistication ('neat and trimly dressed, / Fresh as a bridegroom ... perfumed like a milliner', says Hotspur of such a man in *1 Henry IV*, I.3.33–6) is contrasted with plain-speaking integrity: Oswald is set against Kent in *King Lear*.

When thinking of these matters, we should remember that stage plays were subject to censorship, and any criticism had therefore to be muted or oblique: direct criticism of the monarch or contemporary English court would not be tolerated. This has something to do with why Shakespeare's plays are always set either in the past, or abroad.

The nationalism of the English Renaissance was reinforced by Protestantism. Henry VIII had broken with Rome in the 1530s and in Shakespeare's time there was an independent Protestant state church. Because the Pope in Rome had excommunicated Queen Elizabeth as a heretic and relieved the English of their allegiance to the crown, there was deep suspicion of Roman Catholics as potential traitors. This was enforced by the attempted invasion of the Spanish Armada in 1588. This was a religiously inspired crusade to overthrow Elizabeth and restore England to Roman Catholic allegiance. Roman Catholicism was hence easily identified with hostility to England. Its association with disloyalty and treachery was then reinforced by the Gunpowder Plot of 1605, a Roman Catholic attempt to destroy the government of England.

Shakespeare's plays are remarkably free from direct religious sentiment, but their emphases are Protestant. Young women, for example, are destined for marriage, not for nunneries (precisely what Isabella appears to escape at the end of *Measure for Measure*); friars are dubious characters, full of schemes and deceptions, if with benign intentions, as in *Much Ado About Nothing* or *Romeo and Juliet*. (We should add that Puritans, extreme Protestants, are even less kindly treated than Roman Catholics: for example, Malvolio in *Twelfth Night*).

The central figures of the plays are frequently individuals beset by temptation, by the lure of evil – Angelo in *Measure for Measure*,

CHECK THE FILM
We can get a modern equivalent of the effect of this displacement from Christine Edzard's film of *As You Like It* (1992). Here, the court scenes are set in the luxurious headquarters of a bank or company; the woodland scenes amid a sort of 'cardboard city' of social outcasts and the vulnerable.

Othello, Lear, Macbeth – and not only in tragedies: Falstaff is described as 'that old white-bearded Satan' (*1 Henry IV*, II.4.454). We follow their inner struggles. Shakespeare's heroes have the preoccupation with self and the introspective tendencies encouraged by Protestantism: his tragic heroes are haunted by their consciences, seeking their true selves, agonising over what course of action to take as they follow what can often be understood as a kind of spiritual progress towards heaven or hell.

SHAKESPEARE'S THEATRE

CHECK THE NET
Find out more about the Shakespearean theatre at **http:// www.reading.ac. uk/globe**. This web site describes the historical researches undertaken in connection with the Globe theatre on London's Bankside, which was rebuilt in the late 1990s.

The theatre for which the plays were written was one of the most remarkable innovations of the Renaissance. There had been no theatres or acting companies during the medieval period. Performed on carts and in open spaces at Christian festivals, plays had been almost exclusively religious. Such professional actors as there were wandered the country putting on a variety of entertainments in the yards of inns, on makeshift stages in market squares, or anywhere else suitable. They did not perform full-length plays, but mimes, juggling and comedy acts. Such actors were regarded by officialdom and polite society as little better than vagabonds and layabouts.

Just before Shakespeare went to London all this began to change. A number of young men who had been to the universities of Oxford and Cambridge came to London in the 1580s and began to write plays that made use of what they had learned about the classical drama of ancient Greece and Rome. Plays such as John Lyly's *Alexander and Campaspe* (1584), Christopher Marlowe's *Tamburlaine the Great* (about 1587) and Thomas Kyd's *The Spanish Tragedy* (1588–9) were unlike anything that had been written in English before. They were full-length plays on secular subjects, taking their plots from history and legend, adopting many of the devices of Classical drama, and offering a range of characterisation and situation hitherto unattempted in English drama. With the exception of Lyly's prose dramas, they were composed in the unrhymed iambic pentameters (blank verse), which the Earl of Surrey had introduced into English earlier in the sixteenth century. This was a freer and more expressive medium than the rhymed verse of medieval drama. It was the drama of these 'university wits' that Shakespeare challenged when he came to London. Greene was one of them, and we have heard how little he liked Shakespeare setting himself up as a dramatist.

The most significant change of all, however, was that these dramatists wrote for the professional theatre. In 1576 James Burbage built the first permanent theatre in England, in Shoreditch, just beyond London's northern boundary. It was called simply 'The Theatre'. Others soon followed. Thus, when Shakespeare came to London, there was a flourishing drama, theatres and companies of actors waiting for him, such as there had never been before in England. His company performed at James Burbage's Theatre until 1596, and used the Swan and Curtain until they moved into their own new theatre, the Globe, in 1599. It was burned down in 1613 when a cannon was fired during a performance of Shakespeare's *Henry VIII*.

With the completion in 1996 of Sam Wanamaker's project to construct in London a replica of the Globe, and with productions now running there, a version of Shakespeare's theatre can be experienced at first hand. It is very different to the usual modern experience of drama. The form of the Elizabethan theatre derived from the inn yards and animal baiting rings in which actors had been accustomed to perform in the past. They were circular wooden buildings with a paved courtyard in the middle open to the sky. A rectangular stage jutted out into the middle of this yard. Some of the audience stood in the yard (or 'pit') to watch the play. They were thus on three sides of the stage, close up to it and on a level with it. These 'groundlings' paid only a penny to get in, but for wealthier spectators there were seats in three covered tiers or galleries between the inner and outer walls of the building, extending round most of the auditorium and overlooking the pit and the stage. Such a theatre could hold about 3,000 spectators. The yards were about 80ft in diameter and the rectangular stage approximately 40ft by 30ft and 5ft 6in high. Shakespeare aptly called such a theatre a 'wooden O' in the prologue to *Henry V* (line 13).

The stage itself was partially covered by a roof or canopy, which projected from the wall at the rear of the stage and was supported

CHECK THE BOOK

The most authoritative book on what we know about the theatre of Shakespeare's time is Andrew Gurr's *The Shakespearean Stage* (1992).

CONTEXT

Whereas now, we would conceptualise a visit to the theatre as going to *see* a play, the most common Elizabethan phrase was 'to go *hear* a play' (as in *The Taming of the Shrew*, Induction 2.130) – thus registering the different sensory priorities of the early modern theatre.

THE GLOBE THEATRE,

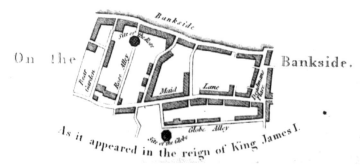

On the Bankside.

As it appeared in the reign of King James I.

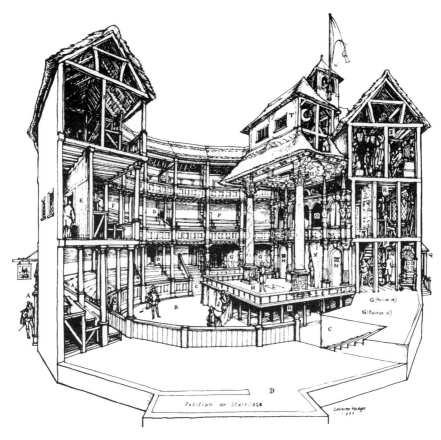

A CONJECTURAL RECONSTRUCTION OF THE INTERIOR OF THE GLOBE PLAYHOUSE

AA Main entrance
B   The Yard
CC Entrances to lowest galleries
D   Entrance to staircase and upper galleries
E   Corridor serving the different sections of the
    middle gallery
F   Middle gallery ('Twopenny Rooms')
G   'Gentlemen's Rooms or Lords Rooms'
H   The stage
J   The hanging being put up round the stage
K   The 'Hell' under the stage
L   The stage trap, leading down to the Hell
MM Stage doors

N   Curtained 'place behind the stage'
O   Gallery above the stage, used as required
    sometimes by musicians, sometimes by
    spectators, and often as part of the play
P   Back-stage area (the tiring-house)
Q   Tiring-house door
R   Dressing-rooms
S   Wardrobe and storage
T   The hut housing the machine for lowering
    enthroned gods, etc., to the stage
U   The 'Heavens'
W   Hoisting the playhouse flag

CONTEXT

We do not know much about the props list for a theatre company in Shakespeare's time, although the evidence we do have suggests that there were some quite ambitious examples: one list dating from 1598 includes decorated cloths depicting cities or the night sky, items of armour, horses' heads and 'one hell mouth', probably for performances of Marlowe's famous play *Doctor Faustus*.

by two posts at the front. This protected the stage and performers from inclement weather, and to it were secured winches and other machinery for stage effects. On either side at the back of the stage was a door. These led into the dressing room (or 'tiring house') and it was by means of these doors that actors entered and left the stage. Between these doors was a small recess or alcove which was curtained off. Such a 'discovery place' served, for example, for Juliet's bedroom when in Act IV Scene 4 of *Romeo and Juliet* the Nurse went to the back of the stage and drew the curtain to find Juliet apparently dead on her bed. Above the discovery place was a balcony, used for the famous balcony scenes of *Romeo and Juliet* (II.2 and III.5), or for the battlements of Richard's castle when he is confronted by Bolingbroke in *Richard II* (III.3). Actors (all parts in the Elizabethan theatre were taken by boys or men) had access to the area beneath the stage; from here, in the 'cellarage', would have come the voice of the ghost of Hamlet's father (*Hamlet*, II.1.150–82).

On these stages there was very little in the way of scenery or props – there was nowhere to store them (there were no wings in this theatre) nor any way to set them up (no tabs across the stage), and, anyway, productions had to be transportable for performance at court or at noble houses. The stage was bare, which is why characters often tell us where they are: there was nothing on the stage to indicate location. It is also why location is so rarely topographical, and much more often symbolic. It suggests a dramatic mood or situation, rather than a place: Lear's barren heath reflects his destitute state, as the storm his emotional turmoil.

None of the plays printed in Shakespeare's lifetime marks act or scene divisions. These have been introduced by later editors, but they should not mislead us into supposing that there was any break in Elizabethan performances such as might happen today while the curtains are closed and the set is changed. The staging of Elizabethan plays was continuous, with the many short 'scenes' of which Shakespeare's plays are often constructed following one after another in quick succession. We have to think of a more fluid, and much faster, production than we are generally used to: in the prologues to *Romeo and Juliet* (line 12) and *Henry VIII* (line 13)

Shakespeare speaks of the playing time as only two hours. It is because plays were staged continuously that exits and entrances are written in as part of the script: characters speak as they enter or leave the stage because otherwise there would be a silence while, in full view, they took up their positions. (This is also why dead bodies have to be carried off: they cannot get up and walk off.)

In 1608 Shakespeare's company, the King's Men, acquired the Blackfriars Theatre, a smaller, rectangular indoor theatre, holding about 700 people, with seats for all the members of the audience, facilities for elaborate stage effects and, because it was enclosed, artificial lighting. It has been suggested that the plays written for this 'private' theatre differed from those written for the Globe, since, as it cost more to go to a private theatre, the audience came from a higher social stratum and demanded the more elaborate and courtly entertainment which Shakespeare's romances provide. However, the King's Men continued to play at the Globe in the summer, using Blackfriars in the winter, and it is not certain that Shakespeare's last plays were written specifically for the Blackfriars theatre, or first performed there.

READING SHAKESPEARE

Shakespeare's plays were written for this stage, but there is also a sense in which they were written *by* the stage. The material and physical circumstances of their production in such theatres had a profound effect upon the nature of Elizabethan plays. Unless we bear this in mind, we are likely to find them very strange, for we will read with expectations shaped by our own familiarity with modern fiction and modern drama which is, by and large, realistic; it seeks to persuade us that what we are reading or watching is really happening. This is quite foreign to Shakespeare. If we try to read him like this, we shall find ourselves irritated by the improbabilities of his plot, confused by his chronology, puzzled by locations, frustrated by unanswered questions and dissatisfied by the motivation of the action. The absurd ease with which disguised persons pass through Shakespeare's plays is a case in point: why does no one recognise people they know so well? There is a great deal of psychological accuracy in Shakespeare's plays, but we are far from any attempt at realism.

 CHECK THE BOOK
Deborah Cartmell's *Interpreting Shakespeare on Screen* (2000) is recommended for its clear and interesting sense of the possibilities and the requirements of approaching Shakespeare through the cinema.

CONTEXT

The Romantic critic S. T. Coleridge argued that literature requires our 'willing suspension of disbelief': but it is not clear that the theatre of the Shakespearean period did require its audience to forget that they were in a theatre. Certainly, remarks calling attention to the theatrical setting are commonplace – in comedies such as *Twelfth Night* (III.4.125) and *As You Like It* II.7.139–43, and in tragedies including *Macbeth* (V.5.23–5) – making it more difficult to forget the theatricality of the stories depicted.

The reason is that in Shakespeare's theatre it was impossible to pretend that the audience was not watching a contrived performance. In a modern theatre, the audience is encouraged to forget itself as it becomes absorbed by the action on stage. The worlds of the spectators and of the actors are sharply distinguished by the lighting: in the dark auditorium the audience is passive, silent, anonymous, receptive and attentive; on the lighted stage the actors are active, vocal, demonstrative and dramatic. (The distinction is, of course, still more marked in the cinema.) There is no communication between the two worlds: for the audience to speak would be interruptive; for the actors to address the audience would be to break the illusion of the play. In the Elizabethan theatre, this distinction did not exist, and for two reasons: first, performances took place in the open air and in daylight which illuminated everyone equally; secondly, the spectators were all around the stage (and wealthier spectators actually on it), and were dressed no differently from the actors, who wore contemporary dress. In such a theatre, spectators would be as aware of each other as of the actors; they could not lose their identity in a corporate group, nor could they ever forget that they were spectators at a performance. There was no chance that they could believe 'this is really happening'.

This, then, was communal theatre, not only in the sense that it was going on in the middle of a crowd but also in the sense that the crowd joined in. Elizabethan audiences had none of our deference: they did not keep quiet, nor arrive on time, nor remain for the whole performance. They joined in, interrupted, even getting on the stage. And plays were preceded and followed by jigs and clowning. It was all much more like our experience of a pantomime, and at a pantomime we are fully aware, and are meant to be aware, that we are watching games being played with reality. The conventions of pantomime revel in their own artificiality: the fishnet tights are to signal that the handsome prince is a woman, the Dame's monstrous false breasts signal that 'she' is a man.

Something very similar is the case with Elizabethan theatre: it utilised its very theatricality. Instead of trying to persuade spectators that they are not in a theatre watching a performance,

Elizabethan plays acknowledge the presence of the audience. It is addressed not only by prologues, epilogues and choruses, but also in soliloquies. There is no realistic reason why characters should suddenly explain themselves to empty rooms, but, of course, there is no empty room. The actor is surrounded by people. Soliloquies are not addressed to the world of the play; they are for the audience's benefit. And that audience's complicity is assumed: when a character like Prospero declares himself to be invisible, it is accepted that he is. Disguises are taken to be impenetrable, however improbable, and we are to accept impossibly contrived situations, such as barely hidden characters remaining undetected (indeed, on the Elizabethan stage there was nowhere at all they could hide).

These, then, are plays that are aware of themselves as dramas; in critical terminology, they are self-reflexive, commenting upon themselves as dramatic pieces and prompting the audience to think about the theatrical experience. They do this not only through their direct address to the audience but also through their fondness for the play-within-a-play (which reminds the audience that the encompassing play is also a play) and their constant use of images from, and allusions to, the theatre. They are fascinated by role-playing, by acting, appearance and reality. Things are rarely what they seem, either in comedy (for example, in *A Midsummer Night's Dream*) or tragedy (*Romeo and Juliet*). This offers one way to think about those disguises: they are thematic rather than realistic. Kent's disguise in *Lear* reveals his true, loyal self, while Edmund, who is not disguised, hides his true self. In *As You Like It*, Rosalind is more truly herself disguised as a man than when dressed as a woman.

The effect of all this is to confuse the distinction we would make between 'real life' and 'acting'. The case of Rosalind, for example, raises searching questions about gender roles, about how far it is 'natural' to be womanly or manly: how does the stage, on which a man can play a woman playing a man (and have a man fall in love with him/her), differ from life, in which we assume the roles we think appropriate to masculine and feminine behaviour? The same is true of political roles: when a Richard II or Lear is so aware of the regal part he is performing, of the trappings and rituals of kingship,

CHECK THE NET
The 'Designing Shakespeare' database at PADS (**www.pads.ahds. ac.uk**) has an extensive collection of photographs from different productions available online.

The poet Walter Raleigh wrote a poem on this image of life as theatre, which begins 'What is our life? A play of passion', in which 'our mothers' wombs the tiring houses be / When we are dressed for this short comedy'. There's a twist at the end of the short verse: 'only we die in earnest, that's no jest'.

their plays raise the uncomfortable possibility that the answer to the question of what constitutes a successful king is simply: a good actor. Indeed, human life generally is repeatedly rendered through the imagery of the stage, from Macbeth's 'Life's but a walking shadow, a poor player / That struts and frets his hour upon the stage / And then is heard no more' (V.5.23–5) to Prospero's paralleling of human life to a performance which, like the globe (both world and theatre!) will end (IV.I.146–58). When life is a fiction, like this play, or this play is a fiction like life, what is the difference? 'All the world's a stage...' (*As You Like It*, II.7.139).

CHRONOLOGY

World events	Shakespeare's life *(dates for plays are approximate)*	Literature and the arts
1492 Columbus sails to America		
		1513 Niccolò Machiavelli, *The Prince*
1534 Henry VIII breaks with Rome and declares himself head of the Church of England		
1556 Archbishop Cranmer burnt at the stake		
1558 Elizabeth I accedes to throne		
	1564 Born in Stratford-upon-Avon	
1568 Mary Queen of Scots taken prisoner by Elizabeth I		
1570 Elizabeth I excommunicated by Pope Pius V		
1571 The Battle of Lepanto		
		1574-87 John Higgins, *A Mirror for Magistrates*
1577 Francis Drake sets out on round the world voyage		**1577** Holinshead, *Chronicles of England, Scotland and Ireland*
		1581 Sir Philip Sidney, *Arcadia*
1582 Outbreak of the plague in London	**1582** Marries Anne Hathaway	
	1583 His daughter, Susanna, is born	
1584 Raleigh's sailors land in Virginia		

continued

World events	Shakespeare's life _(dates for plays are approximate)_	Literature and the arts
	1585 His twins, Hamnet and Judith, are born	
	late 1580s-early 90s Probably writes _Henry VI (Parts I, II, III)_ and _Richard III_	
	c1585-92 Moves to London	
1587 Execution of Mary Queen of Scots after implication in plot to murder Elizabeth I		**1587** Christopher Marlowe, _Tamburlaine the Great_
1588 The Spanish Armada defeated		
1589 Accession of Henri IV to French throne		
		1590 Edmund Spenser, _The Faerie Queene (Books I-III)_
1592 The plague in London closes theatres		
	1593 Writes _Titus Andronicus_	
	1594 onwards Writes exclusively for the Lord Chamberlain's Men; writes _Richard II_	**1594** First performance of _The True Chronicle History of King Leir_
	1595 Writes _Romeo and Juliet_	
1596 Drake perishes on expedition to West Indies	**1596** Hamnet dies; William granted coat of arms	
	1599 Buys shares in the Globe Theatre; writes _Julius Caesar_	
	1600 _The Merchant of Venice_ printed	
	1600-1 Writes _Hamlet_	

World events	Shakespeare's life *(dates for plays are approximate)*	Literature and the arts
1603 Death of Queen Elizabeth I	**1603** onwards His acting company enjoys the patronage of James I as The King's Men	
	1604 *Othello* performed	
1605 Discovery of Guy Fawkes's plot to blow up the Houses of Parliament	**1605** First version of *King Lear*	**1605** Cervantes, *Don Quijote de la Mancha*
	1606 Writes *Macbeth*	
	1606-7 Probably writes *Antony and Cleopatra*	
	1607 Writes *Corialanus, Timon of Athens*	
	1608 The King's Men acquire Blackfriars Theatre for winter performances	
1609 Galileo constructs first astronomical telescope	**1609** Becomes part-owner of the new Blackfriars Theatre	
1610 Henri IV of France assassinated; William Harvey discovers circulation of blood; Galileo observes Saturn for the first time		
	1611 *Cymbeline, The Winter's Tale* and *The Tempest* performed	
1612 Last burning of heretics in England		
	1613 Globe Theatre burns down	
	1616 Dies	
1618 Raleigh executed for treason; Thirty Years War begins in England		
		1622 Birth of French dramatist Molière

THE TEXT AND ITS SOURCES

G.K. Hunter, ed., *King Lear*, The New Penguin Shakespeare, Penguin Books, 1972
   This is the edition of the text used in the preparation of these Notes. It includes full comments on the text itself, helpful notes on the Quarto and Folio texts of *King Lear* and an interesting discussion of the play in the introduction

Kenneth Muir, ed., *King Lear*, The Arden Shakespeare, Methuen, 1959
   The Arden edition of King Lear includes extensive annotations, extracts from sources used by Shakespeare in the appendices and a fine and comprehensive introduction to the play

Kenneth Muir, *King Lear: Penguin Critical Studies*, Penguin Books, 1986
   For a full discussion of Shakespeare's sources for *King Lear*, the section called 'The Making of the Play' is excellent

Gary Taylor and Stanley Wells, eds, *The Complete Works*, Clarendon Press, 1986
   The Quarto and Folio texts of King Lear are printed separately and the editors provide a detailed discussion of their histories. There is also a compact edition of *The Complete Works*, published in 1988

CRITICISM

This list represents only a very small tip of an enormous critical iceberg. Collections of criticism are very useful since they provide a range of views of the play. Some of the best recent collections include:

Susan Bruce, ed., *Shakespeare – King Lear*, (Readers Guides to Essential Criticism), Palgrave Macmillan, 1999
   Traces the development of critical debates about the play, and the ways in which the play has been evaluated and re-evaluated. There are extracts from critics from several centuries

John Drakakis, ed., *Shakespearean Tragedy*, Longman, 1992
   Again, a selection of contemporary views. There are four essays specifically about *King Lear* and other references to the play in other essays. In the introduction Drakakais provides a detailed summary of views about tragedy, which is particularly helpful for undergraduates. The Dollimore essay is reprinted here

William Empson, *Essays on Shakespeare*, Cambridge University Press, 1986
   This gives a reading of the play which offers an unchristian concept of the gods

Frank Kermode, ed., *King Lear: A Casebook*, Macmillan, 1969
   This collection covers a range of criticism of *King Lear* up to the 1960s, including the views of some of the play's early critics

Kiernan Ryan, ed., *King Lear: A Casebook*, New Casebooks, Macmillan, 1993
Concentrates on contemporary criticism of the 1980s. Some essays are less immediately accessible than others, but for a survey of current views this is an excellent selection. Four critics referred to in the section on Critical History – Dollimore, Tennenhouse, Kahn, McCluskie can be found here Ryan provides a helpful explanation of the current trends in literary criticism

Other well-known critics who are worth reading on *King Lear*:

Benedict Anderson, *Imagined Communities*, Verso Books, 1991

Harold Bloom ed., *King Lear*, (Bloom's Reviews: Comprehensive Research and Study Guides), Chelsea House Publishers, 1999

A.C. Bradley, *Shakespearean Tragedy*, 3rd edition, ed. by J.R. Brown, Macmillan, 1992
An influential critic from the beginning of the twentieth century, Bradley focuses on character and motivation

Deborah Cartmell, *Interpreting Shakespeare on Screen*, Palgrave, 2000

Linda Cookson and Bryan Loughrey, *Critical Essays on King Lear*, Longman Critical Essays, Longman, 1988
For a selection of essays including different approaches to the play, written specifically for A-Level students

W.R. Elton, *King Lear and the Gods*, San Marino, California, 1966
For a full discussion of religion and religious attitudes in the play

Rex Gibson, *Shakespearean and Jacobean Tragedy*, (Cambridge Contexts in Literature), Cambridge University Press, 2001
Explores the contextual study of texts by concentrating on a key period. The author aims to aid the understanding of literary, historical and social contexts

Harley Granville-Barker, *Prefaces to Shakespeare II*, London, 1927, reissued in 1982
As a playwright and director, Granville-Barker provides useful insight into staging Shakespeare's plays

Jan Kott, *Shakespeare Our Contemporary*, Cambridge University Press, 1964
Provides a bleak, existentialist reading of the view of humanity portrayed in the play

Alistair McCallum, *King Lear*, (The Shakespeare Handbooks), Ivan R. Dee Inc, 2001

Claire McEachern, *The Cambridge Companion to Shakespearean Tragedy*, Cambridge University Press, 2003

John Russell Brown, *Shakespeare: The Tragedies*, Palgrave, 2001
There are two chapters on the play, covering themes, characters and the two plots

Kiernan Ryan ed., *Shakespeare: Texts and Contexts*, Macmillan, 2000
> There is an excellent chapter on the play by Graham Martin and Stephen Regan, who consider *King Lear* from a variety of angles in an accessible way. There are sections on the plot, the double plot, themes, characters, madness, nature, power and morality, the historical context of the play, religious interpretations of the play, gender and performance. Also includes images of some productions. Highly recommended

Gamini Salgado, *King Lear: Text and Performance*, Macmillan, 1993
> The book is split into two sections – text and performance. Topics covered include the world of the play, dramatic style and structure, conceptions of character and relationships, settings and costumes

G. Wilson Knight, *The Wheel of Fire*, 4th edition, Routledge, 1989
> Includes two fine essays, '*King Lear* and the Comedy of the Grotesque' and 'The *Lear* universe'

SHAKESPEARE'S THEATRE

For anyone interested in the history of the Elizabethan playhouses, staging practices and acting companies the following book is invaluable:

Andrew Gurr, *The Shakespearean Stage*, Cambridge University Press, 1992

SHAKESPEARE'S LIFE

Samuel Schoenbaum, *Shakespeare: A Documentary Life*, Oxford University Press, 1975

alliteration a sequence of repeated consonantal sounds in a stretch of language. The matching consonants are usually at the beginning of words or stressed syllables. See for example the repeated 'd' in Kent's lines in Act V, 'All's cheerless, dark, and deadly. / Your eldest daughters have fordone themselves, / And desperately are dead.' (V.3.288–90)

Aristotle a Greek philosopher (384–322BC), whose Poetics (observations about Tragedy collected by his followers) is an early and influential example of empirical criticism. By the examination of examples Aristotle attempts to analyse those features that make some tragedies more successful than others. He focuses on the nature of the plot and its connections with a moral pattern, the typifying features of the tragic hero, and the play's intensity of focus in time and place (later called the Unities)

aside an aside is a common dramatic convention in which a character speaks in such a way that some of the characters on stage do not hear what is said, while others do. It may also be a direct address to the audience, revealing the character's views, thoughts, motives and intentions

blank verse unrhymed iambic pentameter: a line of five iambs.

characterisation the way in which a writer creates characters so as to attract or repel our sympathy. Different kinds of literature have certain conventions of characterisation. In Jacobean drama there were many stock dramatic 'types' (see Machiavellian, malcontent) whose characteristics were familiar to the audience

chorus in the tragedies of the ancient Greek playwrights the 'chorus' is a group of characters who represent the ordinary people in their attitudes to the action which they witness as bystanders, and on which they comment. The Fool is in some ways a choral character, who comments as an observer on the action of the play. The choral character is not a major participant in the events witnessed, but his comments are full of ironic insight

closure the impression of completeness and finality achieved by the ending of some literary works: 'and they all lived happily ever after'. *King Lear* is now seen as a play which defies closure; it refuses to leave the reader or audience with a feeling of comfortable satisfaction. It is hard to reach conclusive judgements about many issues in *King Lear*

denouement the final unfolding of a plot: the point at which the reader's expectations, be they hopes or fears, about what will happen to the characters are finally satisfied or denied

dramatic irony a feature of many plays: it occurs when the development of the plot allows the audience to possess more information about what is happening than some of the characters themselves have. Characters may also speak in a dramatically ironic way, saying something that points to events to come without understanding the significance of their words

feminist feminism is, broadly speaking, a political movement claiming political and economic equality of women with men. Feminist criticism and scholarship seek to explore or expose the masculine 'bias' in texts and challenge traditional ideas about them, constructing and then offering a feminine perspective on works of art. Since the late 1960s feminist theories about literature and language, and feminist interpretations of texts have multiplied enormously. Feminism has its roots in previous centuries; early texts championing women's rights include Mary Wollstonecraft's *A Vindication of the Rights of Women* (1792) and J.S. Mill's *The Subjection of Women* (1869)

humanism the humanists' attitude to the world is anthropocentric: instead of regarding man as a fallen, corrupt and sinful creature, their idea of truth and excellence is based on human values and human experience. They strive for moderate, achievable, even worldly aims, rather than revering asceticism. 'Humanism' in a general sense has been revived at various times since the Renaissance. Nowadays 'humanism' refers vaguely to moral philosophies which reject the supernatural beliefs of religion

imagery the figurative language in a piece of literature (**metaphors** and similes); or all the words which refer to objects and qualities which appeal to the senses and feelings

Machiavellian the Machiavel was a villainous stock character in Elizabethan and Jacobean drama, so called after the Florentine writer Niccolo Machiavelli (1469–1527), author of *The Prince* (written 1513), a book of political advice to rulers that recommended the need under certain circumstances to lie to the populace for their own good and to preserve power. Embellishment of this suggestion (which was only one small part of his analysis of political power and justice) made Machiavelli almost synonymous with the Devil in English literature. Machiavels are practised liars and cruel political opportunists, who delight in their own manipulative evil. The topic of dissembling and disguising one's true identity amount almost to an obsession in plays in the early seventeenth century

malcontent the malcontent was a familiar figure in Jacobean drama; sometimes a tragic hero e.g. *Hamlet*, but not necessarily so. It meant being disaffected, melancholy, dissatisfied with or disgusted by society and life. Edmund is not a true malcontent, although he shares some of the characteristics described here. He is unhappy with his position in life and on the fringes of society, which he mocks and seeks to undermine

metaphor a metaphor goes further than a comparison between two different things or ideas by fusing them together: one thing is described as being another thing, thus 'carrying over' all its associations.

new historicist the new historicism refers to the work of a loose affiliation of critics who discuss literary works in terms of their historical contexts. In particular, they seek to study literature as part of a wider cultural history, exploring the relationship of literature to society

pathos moments in works of art which evoke strong feelings of pity are said to have this quality

poetic justice the idea that literature should always depict a world in which virtue and vice are eventually rewarded and punished appropriately. The deaths of the evil characters in *King Lear* can be viewed as examples of poetic justice

soliloquy a curious but fascinating dramatic convention, which allows a character in a play to speak directly to the audience, as if thinking aloud about motives, feelings and decisions. The psychological depth which the soliloquy gives to Shakespeare's tragedies is inestimable. Part of the convention is that a soliloquy provides accurate access to the character's innermost thoughts: we learn more about the character than could ever be gathered from the action of the play alone

tragedy A tragedy traces the career and downfall of an individual, and shows in the downfall both the capacities and the limitations of human life. The protagonist may be superhuman, a monarch or, in the modern age, an ordinary person

Rebecca Warren teaches English. She is the author of York Notes Advanced on *King Lear*, *The Taming of the Shrew*, *Richard III*, *The Mayor of Casterbridge*, *Sylvia Plath's Selected Poems* and *The Glass Menagerie*.

General editors

Martin Gray, former Head of the Department of English Studies at the University of Stirling, and of Literary Studies at the University of Luton

Professor A. N. Jeffares, Emeritus Professor of English, University of Stirling

Maya Angelou
I Know Why the Caged Bird Sings

Jane Austen
Pride and Prejudice

Alan Ayckbourn
Absent Friends

Elizabeth Barrett Browning
Selected Poems

Robert Bolt
A Man for All Seasons

Harold Brighouse
Hobson's Choice

Charlotte Brontë
Jane Eyre

Emily Brontë
Wuthering Heights

Shelagh Delaney
A Taste of Honey

Charles Dickens
David Copperfield
Great Expectations
Hard Times
Oliver Twist

Roddy Doyle
Paddy Clarke Ha Ha Ha

George Eliot
Silas Marner
The Mill on the Floss

Anne Frank
The Diary of a Young Girl

William Golding
Lord of the Flies

Oliver Goldsmith
She Stoops to Conquer

Willis Hall
The Long and the Short and the Tall

Thomas Hardy
Far from the Madding Crowd
The Mayor of Casterbridge
Tess of the d'Urbervilles
The Withered Arm and other Wessex Tales

L.P. Hartley
The Go-Between

Seamus Heaney
Selected Poems

Susan Hill
I'm the King of the Castle

Barry Hines
A Kestrel for a Knave

Louise Lawrence
Children of the Dust

Harper Lee
To Kill a Mockingbird

Laurie Lee
Cider with Rosie

Arthur Miller
The Crucible
A View from the Bridge

Robert O'Brien
Z for Zachariah

Frank O'Connor
My Oedipus Complex and Other Stories

George Orwell
Animal Farm

J.B. Priestley
An Inspector Calls
When We Are Married

Willy Russell
Educating Rita
Our Day Out

J.D. Salinger
The Catcher in the Rye

William Shakespeare
Henry IV Part I
Henry V
Julius Caesar
Macbeth
The Merchant of Venice
A Midsummer Night's Dream
Much Ado About Nothing

Romeo and Juliet
The Tempest
Twelfth Night

George Bernard Shaw
Pygmalion

Mary Shelley
Frankenstein

R.C. Sherriff
Journey's End

Rukshana Smith
Salt on the snow

John Steinbeck
Of Mice and Men

Robert Louis Stevenson
Dr Jekyll and Mr Hyde

Jonathan Swift
Gulliver's Travels

Robert Swindells
Daz 4 Zoe

Mildred D. Taylor
Roll of Thunder, Hear My Cry

Mark Twain
Huckleberry Finn

James Watson
Talking in Whispers

Edith Wharton
Ethan Frome

William Wordsworth
Selected Poems

A Choice of Poets

Mystery Stories of the Nineteenth Century including The Signalman

Nineteenth Century Short Stories

Poetry of the First World War

Six Women Poets

For the AQA Anthology:

Duffy and Armitage & Pre-1914 Poetry

Heaney and Clarke & Pre-1914 Poetry

Poems from Different Cultures

Margaret Atwood
Cat's Eye
The Handmaid's Tale

Jane Austen
Emma
Mansfield Park
Persuasion
Pride and Prejudice
Sense and Sensibility

Alan Bennett
Talking Heads

William Blake
Songs of Innocence and of Experience

Charlotte Brontë
Jane Eyre
Villette

Emily Brontë
Wuthering Heights

Angela Carter
Nights at the Circus

Geoffrey Chaucer
The Franklin's Prologue and Tale
The Merchant's Prologue and Tale
The Miller's Prologue and Tale
The Prologue to the Canterbury Tales
The Wife of Bath's Prologue and Tale

Samuel Coleridge
Selected Poems

Joseph Conrad
Heart of Darkness

Daniel Defoe
Moll Flanders

Charles Dickens
Bleak House
Great Expectations
Hard Times

Emily Dickinson
Selected Poems

John Donne
Selected Poems

Carol Ann Duffy
Selected Poems

George Eliot
Middlemarch
The Mill on the Floss

T.S. Eliot
Selected Poems
The Waste Land

F. Scott Fitzgerald
The Great Gatsby

E.M Forster
A Passage to India

Brian Friel
Translations

Thomas Hardy
Jude the Obscure
The Mayor of Casterbridge
The Return of the Native
Selected Poems
Tess of the d'Urbervilles

Seamus Heaney
Selected Poems from 'Opened Ground'

Nathaniel Hawthorne
The Scarlet Letter

Homer
The Iliad
The Odyssey

Aldous Huxley
Brave New World

Kazuo Ishiguro
The Remains of the Day

Ben Jonson
The Alchemist

James Joyce
Dubliners

John Keats
Selected Poems

Philip Larkin
The Whitsun Weddings and Selected Poems

Christopher Marlowe
Doctor Faustus
Edward II

Arthur Miller
Death of a Salesman

John Milton
Paradise Lost Books I & II

Toni Morrison
Beloved

George Orwell
Nineteen Eighty-Four

Sylvia Plath
Selected Poems

Alexander Pope
Rape of the Lock & Selected Poems

William Shakespeare
Antony and Cleopatra
As You Like It
Hamlet
Henry IV Part I
King Lear
Macbeth
Measure for Measure
The Merchant of Venice
A Midsummer Night's Dream
Much Ado About Nothing
Othello
Richard II
Richard III
Romeo and Juliet
The Taming of the Shrew
The Tempest
Twelfth Night
The Winter's Tale

George Bernard Shaw
Saint Joan

Mary Shelley
Frankenstein

Jonathan Swift
Gulliver's Travels and A Modest Proposal

Alfred Tennyson
Selected Poems

Virgil
The Aeneid

Alice Walker
The Color Purple

Oscar Wilde
The Importance of Being Earnest

Tennessee Williams
A Streetcar Named Desire
The Glass Menagerie

Jeanette Winterson
Oranges Are Not the Only Fruit

John Webster
The Duchess of Malfi

Virginia Woolf
To the Lighthouse

William Wordsworth
The Prelude and Selected Poems

W.B. Yeats
Selected Poems

Metaphysical Poets